The
Reading/Writing
Teacher's
Companion

BUILD
A LITERATE
CLASSROOM

The Reading/Writing Teacher's Companion

Investigate Nonfiction
Experiment with Fiction
Discover Your Own Literacy
Build a Literate Classroom
Explore Poetry (forthcoming)

The
Reading/Writing
Teacher's
Companion

BUILD
A LITERATE
CLASSROOM

Donald H. Graves

HEINEMANN
Portsmouth, NH

IRWIN PUBLISHING
Toronto, Canada

Heinemann Educational Books, Inc.

361 Hanover Street   Portsmouth, NH 03801-3959
Offices and agents throughout the world

Published simultaneously in Canada by
Irwin Publishing

1800 Steeles Avenue West   Concord, Ontario, Canada L4K 2P3

Figure 10–5: From Donald H. Graves, *Writing: Teachers and Children at Work*. Portsmouth, NH: Heinemann, 1983, p. 185. Reprinted by permission.

Every effort has been made to contact the copyright holders for permission to reprint borrowed material. We regret any oversights that may have occurred and would be happy to rectify them in future printings of this work.

Library of Congress Cataloging-in-Publication Data

Graves, Donald H.
    Build a literate classroom / Donald H. Graves.
        p.   cm.—(The Reading/writing teacher's companion)
    Includes bibliographical references (p.   ) and index.
        ISBN 0-435-08488-7
        1. Language arts (Elementary)   2. Classroom environment.   3. Interaction analysis in education.   I. Title.   II. Series: Graves, Donald H. Reading/writing teacher's companion.
LB1576.G72728   1991
372.6—dc20   90-43879
                                                  CIP

Canadian Cataloguing in Publication Data

Graves, Donald H.
    Build a literate classroom

(The Reading/writing teacher's companion)
Includes bibliographical references and index.
ISBN 0-7725-1838-6

1. Language arts (Elementary).   2. Classroom environment.   3. Interaction analysis in education.   I. Title.   II. Series: Graves, Donald H. The reading/writing teacher's companion.

LB1576.G73   1991   372.6   C91-093160-7

Designed by Wladislaw Finne.
Back-cover photo by Mekeel McBride.
Printed in the United States of America.
10 9 8 7 6 5 4 3 2

**To
Jane Hansen**

---

*Colleague in research
and learning*

contents

Action: Practice Directives.
Final Reflection

*Action: Review Your Own Personal Practices in
    Reading and Writing.*
Action: Spot the Lifelong Reader/Writer.
*Action: Establish Portfolios as a Means for More Effective,
    Continuous Evaluation.*
Action: Help Children Keep Good Records.
*Action: Evaluate Children's Ability to Evaluate Their
    Own Work.*
*Action: Establish the Inverted Pyramid Approach to
    Evaluation.*
Action: Evaluate Children's Work with Conventions.
Action: Take a Hard Look at Standardized Tests.
Action: Help Children Learn How to Take Tests.
*Action: Take the Initiative; Share Your Data with
    Administrators.*
*Action: Make Evaluation a Celebration of Learning with
    Children.*
Final Reflection

about this series

Reading and writing are both composing processes. History shows they have been kept apart. This series, The Reading/Writing Teacher's Companion, brings them together. With these books as a guide, you can explore the richness of reading and writing for yourself and for children. You can improve your own listening, experiment with learning, and recognize children's potential in reading and writing. Five books will make up the series:

- *Investigate Nonfiction.*
- *Experiment with Fiction.*
- *Discover Your Own Literacy.*
- *Build a Literate Classroom.*
- *Explore Poetry.*

The approach to teaching and learning is basically the same in all five books, although each stands alone in its focus. All five emphasize a learning style that immediately engages you in trying literacy for yourself, then the children. So much of learning is, and ought to be, experimental. A series of "Actions," experiments for personal growth and discovery in the classroom, are highlighted in the text to help you develop the kind of literate classroom you want. The Actions are ordered in such a way that you will gradually become aware of children's growing independence in some aspect of literacy. In all five books I'll be trying the experiments right along with you.

The five books stress learning within a literate community. Reading and writing are social acts in which children and teachers together share the books and authors they enjoy and their own composing in the various genres. Make no mistake, individuals are important, but good classrooms have always stressed group as well as individual responsibility.

The books also stress the importance of your own learning within a community. When you try the Actions and enter into new experiments with your teaching, you ought to consider reading and learning with colleagues in order to maximize your own efforts to grow as a professional.

acknowl-edgments

I wrote this book over a number of years. Parts of it began in 1985 while I was working at Mast Way School in Lee, New Hampshire. I continued to write it through a three-year study in Stratham, New Hampshire, and while working the last two years in Moultonboro and Conway, New Hampshire. Thus, in the process of writing this book I have learned from many classroom teachers and colleagues.

Through all of these studies I worked with Jane Hansen, my colleague at the University of New Hampshire. Many of these ideas were shared with her in telephone conversations and early drafts. I am grateful for her help in the nine years we have worked together, and this book is dedicated to her.

A number of classroom teachers were especially helpful. As always, they have been my best teachers in the myriad ways they reveal children's potential and advance the teaching of reading and writing. Leslie Funkhouser, now of the A. Scott Crossfield Elementary School in Herndon, Virginia, and Pat McLure, first-grade teacher at the Mast Way School, were important teachers.

Linda Rief, eighth-grade teacher at Oyster River Middle School, contributed much through her classroom research. Mark Milliken, Mary Ann Wessells, Nancy Herdecker, and Chip Nelson, all from Stratham Memorial School, contributed letters, classroom data, and insights into student literacy.

Brenda Miller Power and Ruth Hubbard, co-researchers at Mast Way School, and now professors at the University of Maine and Lewis and Clark College in Oregon, helped me rethink the meaning of children's potential as readers and writers.

Countless children shared their writing and views of literacy. In particular, Xiao Di Fu and Kelsey Taylor opened new doors to my understanding of children's learning potential.

Then there are those colleagues through all five of the books in this series who read, challenge, calm, and advise: Nancie Atwell, Mary Ellen Giacobbe, Don Murray, and Jane Hansen.

Philippa Stratton, my editor at Heinemann, and Donna Bouvier, Manager of Editing and Production, have encouraged and enlarged the vision for this series, as well as provided attention to the necessary details that make a finished product.

I thank Mary Comstock for her response to the skills section, Dan Ling Fu for the very important study of her son, Xiao Di, and the encouragement of Bonnie Sunstein, my doctoral assistant through the last two years of writing the book.

My wife, Betty, has been my most consistent reader. Her ability to give frank, no-nonsense responses to my text, as well as participate in some of the Actions, has been a source of immeasurable help . . . and is not taken for granted.

1

make your own decisions—
with the children

Leslie Funkhouser makes her own decisions. She knows that if she waits for other people to tell her what to do, she and the children she teaches can't share the important decisions that make a literate classroom.

As part of this approach, Leslie delegates broad responsibilities. As a researcher in her classroom, I counted up the responsibilities she had delegated to her second graders that she used to do herself. The total was twenty-two. Children took on these responsibilities because they knew it would result in a better classroom, and it has. The atmosphere is one of "What can I do next" as children industriously pursue their own reading and writing, aware of the role they play in the decision making.

I remember when Leslie decided to introduce trade books on Fridays as an adjunct to the basal reading program.* It wasn't long before she and the children moved from one to three, then five days of trade books. They had discovered that they read more when they took time to read trade books. "How is this working?" Leslie would ask the class, and she expected detailed answers. The children's answers convinced her that trade books deserved more reading time.

Not all the decisions in the classroom are made jointly. When Leslie decided to abolish the homogeneous groups she had maintained during her basal reading program she simply reasoned, "I don't group for writing, why should I group for reading?" She soon found that children who had been in the lower groups read more when they were with better readers and told the class, "We'll have all different kinds of groups when we share our reading."

This book is intended to help you design your own literate classroom. Literate professionals like you and Leslie make im-

* When I first worked with Leslie she taught at the Mast Way School in Lee, New Hampshire. She now teaches at the A. Scott Crossfield Elementary School in Herndon, Virginia.

1

portant decisions about your own literacy and the literacy of the children you teach. Deciding to try something new involves two kinds of discipline—being able to say "yes" and being able to say "no." We all have routines and rhythms to our daily lives, and the decision to experiment affects the other things we do. Deciding to say "yes" usually means we have to say "no" to something else.

DON'T EXPERIMENT ALONE You might as well have company when you try new experiments in your classroom, so why not ask a colleague to go through this book with you? The two of you may not try the same experiments, but you may both discover that pioneering new practices is an energy-producing event of the highest order. At the same time, you will be able to share your readings as well as the bugs that perplex you, and if you are in the same building, you can visit each other's classroom.

As an alternative, don't hesitate to call a colleague-friend in another town to try the experiments with you. At the end of our summer courses at the University of New Hampshire, when the bonds of friendship are especially strong, I recommend that students invest $25 in telephone calls. Since you would spend $25 at the start of a course, why not spend the same amount to continue the course into September as you apply theory and practice in your own classroom?

Involve your students. They are eager to help if you are serious about enlisting their aid. Over the years, I've learned a number of valuable lessons about the power of experimental teaching when students are cooperatively involved.

Linda Rief, an eighth-grade teacher at Oyster River Middle School in Durham, New Hampshire, did a study of the ability of her eighth-grade students to evaluate their own writing. Before she began, she discussed the matter with her students and asked for their help. The students pitched in with enthusiasm. They were used to helping her with other matters, so her frank request for help with more formal research was simply one more opportunity for them to get involved and improve their own classroom.

As her study progressed, Linda shared the data with her students. At her request, they kept records of how they rated the relative quality of their writing, and then they wrote short paragraphs evaluating the best and the poorest pieces. In addition to their record keeping, the students often shared their own informal observations about the study. The final data showed that Linda's students were able to evaluate their writing as well as teachers and professional writers. Not only were the data students collected valuable; their participation ensured that Linda's answer to the question "How well do students learn to evaluate their own writing?" was based on solid information.

Leslie Funkhouser uses another approach in soliciting student participation in the classroom. When things don't go well she expects her students to have some insight into why they don't. On one particular day as I sat in her second-grade classroom recording data, four children gathered around a table to share their books. They each read a favorite part and then the other three children and Leslie responded. The session went poorly. The children did not read well, and during the readings the other three participants continued to read their own books under the table. The question-and-answer session was perfunctory and dealt poorly with the texts the children read. Leslie was clearly upset and cornered one of the participants. "Nicole, that was terrible. What went wrong? I want to know."

"It was *boring*, Ms. Funkhouser. I didn't know when you'd ask us to come for share so I didn't have my piece ready; and when we read it sounded boring. Besides, I was right at a good part in my reading and didn't want to leave."

The information was a little disturbing to Leslie. Still, she realized that the children had a point. She decided to let them know a day in advance when they needed to be ready for group sharing. She knew she could expect more if the children did a better job preparing. Nicole's observation proved correct; the sessions improved.

The following example occurred many years ago, and I can only remember that the teacher's name was Russell. Russell had just returned from a year of teaching in Oxfordshire. His eyes danced as he explained how he involved the children during the first two days of classes.

"I decided the class was as much the children's as mine. In the past I'd set the room up just so, just the way I wanted it. All the aesthetics were set, proper bulletin boards with fine picture backing, art, book, and science centers. I think the children liked the room but actually they hardly noticed what care had gone into it. Well, this year I changed all that. I spoke to the school head and told him I was going to try something new. We'd all work together for two solid days to make the room ours, designing it as we went. At the same time I assured him I'd be able to set a tone for the entire year that would pay off.

"When the children came in that first day, their eyes fairly fell out of their heads. The room was barren. Desks were piled in the center of the room along with cabinets. But I had all kinds of materials for bulletin boards, dividers for marking off the room, science materials, scales, you name it. The only thing in place was the rug way over in the corner of the room. I motioned for all the children to join me on the rug. When they were all seated I said, 'What did you think when you came into the room?' The children expressed their puzzlement in myriad ways.

"I said, well, this is our room and we are going to have the wonderful opportunity to make it ours, build it just the way we'd like. But first let's talk about our vision for the room. (These were ten-year-olds; ten-year-olds love to dream.) Let's talk about what we'd like to learn this year . . . and that includes me, what I'd like to learn. After we talk about what we'd like to learn, we'll talk about how we can set the room up so it'll help us do and become what we'd like together."

Russell and the children shared their love of science and learning, making things, reading books, putting on plays, doing choral speaking, singing, and writing. As the children began to share their ideas, Russell mentioned some theories about room arrangements and discussed such elements as

- Construction areas.
- Science and display areas.
- Performance areas.
- Book access.
- Materials.
- Quiet areas.
- All-class get-together areas.
- Storage areas for children's personal things.

Within several hours the children had divided up into work details to follow sketches of how they wished the room to look. Bulletin boards went up as well as corrugated dividers for displaying work yet to come. Such issues as what work would go up and how everyone could have a contribution to make were discussed. Debates about excellence, the classroom as community, and people helping each other wove through their exchanges. A community was born, and born quickly. All the children had a place in a vision they had begun to create together.

In Mark Milliken's fifth-grade class in Stratham, New Hampshire, the children read about Pizarro in their social studies textbook. One child, who could scarcely contain his anger, bellowed, "What kind of book is this, what kind of authors are these who keep quiet on the injustice of this matter? Nowhere does it say that what Pizarro did to the Incas was wrong."

"Well then," Mark asked, "how would you write it, what information would you need to make it right?" The children worked at finding resources while Mark sat back and became a consultant to a project the children undertook for themselves.

ACTIONS   Although this book was written to help you design your own literate classroom, the problem with any book, including this one, is that the range of its readership is diverse. I cannot anticipate the best place for you to start, so I will provide a series of Actions through which you can experiment with new approaches to teaching. (If you tried some of the approaches Leslie Funkhouser, Linda Rief, Russell, or Mark Milliken used with their students you would be trying what I am calling Actions.) Although I will specify ways to approach each new Action, you can make each experiment your own by adapting it to your own students.

The following chapter synopses give an advance picture of your own involvement as well as the rationale for including each approach in your teaching repertoire. If you wish, read all nine before deciding which is the best starter chapter for you. The chapters and their accompanying Actions are listed here in an order that is loosely based on what teachers have said they need to know before moving to the next set of Actions.

Chapter 2: Rethink learning and the use of time   More and more learning time is taken from us by yearly additions to the school curriculum and by an increasing number of classroom interruptions. In addition, our conception of what constitutes real learning and teaching has been pushed aside by the demand for mere coverage of information and skills. This chapter discusses the need to reformulate learning in light of what our children will need today and in the twenty-first century. It also looks at how we waste time in the classroom and suggests ways to save it.

Chapter 3: Structure a literate classroom   Literacy is a natural act that requires an unnatural environment. If the classroom is not carefully designed and structured by teacher and children, and if it is not continually adapted to meet their shifting needs, then students' natural urge to express themselves will be thwarted. Delegating tasks to children is an essential part of effective structure. The Actions in this chapter show the kinds of tasks that can be delegated. Theories of structure along with common problems in room structure and the need to define and negotiate territory are also discussed.

Chapter 4: What writing does Part of the power of writing lies in what it does and what it can be used for. This chapter provides a series of Actions to help children understand how writing communicates. It considers publication, storing information through record keeping, and reviewing writing composed earlier in the year.

Chapter 5: What reading does Because we take reading for granted, we forget its power. To help ourselves and the children we teach understand the power of reading, this chapter reviews, in a practical way, just how reading enhances the quality of life in the classroom. What is a book? What are the different kinds of books? How do adults use books? How do we use books in the classroom? These are a few of the questions that can help us understand the uniqueness of print and books.

Chapter 6: Shorten conferences In the past, I have placed too much emphasis on the writing/reading conference. Because effective conferences are supported by many other classroom practices, they can be shortened to become more effective. This chapter examines teaching practices that can shorten conferences, selecting children for conferences more effectively, and using delay and referral to other children.

Chapter 7: Connect skills with meaning Frank Smith says that every act in the process of writing is an act of convention. The act of reading requires us to understand how writers use conventions—of grammar, spelling, and punctuation—to enhance meaning. If writers ignore fundamental conventions, readers will not understand the texts they write. This chapter focuses on a mini-lesson approach to conventions. The Actions give examples of children sharing conventions, observing their use by professional writers, and conducting mini-lessons of their own.

Chapter 8: Look for potential

We need a realistic sense of personal potential. In fact, this entire book could be seen as a collection of Actions that are directed toward helping you realize your potential as a professional. When you do, the children in your classroom begin to sense the potential in themselves. This chapter first guides you in looking at your own potential and then introduces Actions to help you examine your students' potential in reading and writing through their knowledge of writing and books and of skills and genres. Additional Actions help you to evaluate children's folders and the records of the books they are reading. Further Actions show you how to help children, particularly those with learning problems, to understand their own potential. The more you recognize their resources, the more you realize your own potential as a professional.

Chapter 9: Raise expectations

This chapter focuses on the hard work necessary to encourage potential. You demonstrate how you challenge yourself as a learner. You expect children to learn when concepts are right for them. When you have high expectations for a particular child because you have worked hard to understand that child's potential, you offer a vote of confidence to the learner—and to yourself as a teacher. This chapter examines different kinds of expectations, from nudging, to recommending, to explicit directives to the child.

Chapter 10: Evaluate your own classroom

Literate classrooms provide many ways to use reading and writing. Few of these uses are represented or examined in standardized assessments, so you need to design your own evaluation program—which can and should be more demanding than traditional approaches because children contribute a large amount of the data and participate in the evaluation process as full-fledged members.

FINAL REFLECTION   Children need to be part of a classroom in which you make decisions. When you experiment in your teaching you show children how you learn. In a natural way, you enlist the children's help in order to build a more effective community of learners.

When you act independently and become aware of your own growth as a professional, you will feel more comfortable about allowing children to experience the same kind of risk taking. Your decisions will be more focused: "I will do more of this. I will do less of that." You can concentrate for a significant period on one aspect of literacy, teaching, or learning until you are ready to decide which Action you want to try next.

*rethink learning and
the use of time*

I am an active person. I make long lists of things to do, check them off, and call it progress. Or so it seems. A friend once observed my lists at day's end and wryly remarked, "Busy man, you've had a little day."

In education we've associated busyness with accomplishment. Students write papers, and we move in a flurry of response from child to child. We cover six curriculum components by 10:00 A.M. and feel the warmth of moral rightness. Folders fill with writing, trade books are checked out regularly, and the children brim with enthusiasm. We stuff every possible moment with teaching and learning and feel right in our actions, yet we wonder. And in our wonder we begin to rethink learning and our use of time.

Take ten minutes to look at your last teaching day and make a quick list of what you did. Examine the list. Then ask a few questions: (1) How significant was each item to a particular child's long-term learning? (2) What were the items that contributed most significantly to learning, and how can you increase these activities?

There, you've opened the door on what learning lasts for children.

This chapter begins in a different way from the others. It begins with Action/Reflections in which you do some background thinking to prepare for Actions in your classroom. I'll try the Action/Reflections along with you.

ACTION/REFLECTION: CONSIDER THE KIND OF LITERATE LEARNER YOU THINK IS NEEDED FOR THE TWENTY-FIRST CENTURY AND DRAW UP A PROFILE OF THAT LEARNER.

If I am going to gain perspective on my teaching today I need to look more carefully at where I am headed. More particularly, I need to look at what I think my students need for the life they will lead. Children in first grade this year (1990) will almost be in college by 2001, and children now in the upper grades

11

will be in the workplace. Both groups will need a kind of literacy that should be described today. I'll list some of the questions I am considering. You can cross out some of mine and add some of your own as you think of your students:

1. Do the children see themselves as reader/writers?
2. Do the children use reading and writing to learn new things?
3. Do the children initiate reading and writing without an assignment?
4. Do the children initiate sharing reading and writing with others?
5. Do the children have plans for the next thing they will read/write or learn?
6. Do the children read and write in a variety of ways, that is, choose different books in different genres?
7. Do the children possess specific knowledge areas or unique ways of expressing their thoughts through art, music, drama, or crafts of various kinds?

These questions obviously reflect my own values about what our children will need in the twenty-first century. The words I use embody them: use, initiate, share, plan, learn, and choose. The people I envision are highly independent learners who act on their own, perceive what needs to be learned, and sustain reading/writing to achieve self-designed ends. They are also able to work with others and handle assigned tasks. At the core of these learners' activities are specific interests and various ways of expressing what they know in various forms of media.

ACTION/REFLECTION: CONSIDER HOW YOU WILL CHANGE YOUR TEACHING OF READING AND WRITING TO ENCOURAGE THE KIND OF LEARNER YOU HAVE PROFILED.

I work for the long haul, changing my teaching to fit how I think children learn. That is, I look for ways to help children become lifelong readers, writers, and thinkers.

A number of learning principles are embedded in my teaching plans for the future:

- Children learn by reading and writing in school for extensive amounts of time. Unless children actually read and write they will not understand what reading and writing are for or gain the skills necessary to become independent learners.
- Children learn the meaning of texts by sharing their work with others in order to receive help, discovering the varied reactions of audiences, and having their work challenged. Reading and writing are social acts.
- Children learn by solving many kinds of problems in order to make their intentions clear. These problems can be as simple as decoding and understanding the meaning of a word, reorganizing a text for clarity, or rereading several sources to select the most accurate information.
- Children learn in an environment that expects challenge. Issues of plausibility abound: "Why did he do that? What is your evidence for that? Show me the actual words that mean that. How did you decide that you had completed this piece, this book?"
- Children learn from our *demonstrations* about reading, writing, and learning. We show how *we* read, write, and solve problems. This means that we regularly read and write with the children.
- Children learn because we demonstrate the use and meaning of many kinds of skills, from how to punctuate, capitalize, and revise a text to understanding how authors handle character and plot in their writing.

- Children learn because they take an active role in their own learning. They learn how to evaluate their own work, plan new learning, and make effective choices in the topics they write about and the books they read.

ACTION/REFLECTION: CONSIDER HOW YOU WILL CHANGE THE WAY YOU USE TIME TO PROVIDE THE BEST TEACHING FOR THE LEARNER OF THE TWENTY-FIRST CENTURY.

Above all, I work to delegate more and more to the children. This means that they take more responsibility for the everyday running of the classroom, the solving of problems (both social and academic), and the evaluation and planning of their work. One way I have changed in my view of how time is used is that I want children to know what to do with it. My new view of time and learning is reflected in some of the following practices:

- Daily work with skills through mini-lessons.
- Rethinking curriculum so that children learn how to learn.
- Treating reading and writing as composing processes and not teaching them separately.
- Working to have reading and writing become applied subjects by using them in mathematics, science, and social studies. Time is saved whenever children are self-engaged in superior kinds of thinking, when reading and writing go to work.
- Including such subjects as handwriting, spelling, and grammar as part of writing and reading.
- Providing sustained work time and negotiating with school administrators to maintain it.
- Helping children to raise big enough questions about their intentions to have something worthwhile to sustain their thinking.

You will think of many other practices you would consider as part of your Action/Reflection. You have probably noticed that some of the following principles help you to use time more efficiently:

• Reduce the number of subjects; embed one in another.
• Put reading and writing to work in other subjects.
• Work for sustained activity with few transitions.
• Focus on independent individual and cooperative thinking.

This chapter is devoted to saving school time while helping children to move to more productive work. We will use Actions first to examine how time is wasted and then to help us save time in order to prepare students to be learners in tomorrow's society.

ACTION: RETHINK THE BEGINNING OF YOUR SCHOOL DAY OR THE BEGINNING OF CLASS.

This is a simple place to begin to rethink how you use time. How well I recall my early years of teaching when I was afraid I would run out of material to teach by recess. I had more trivial things to do to get children started in the day: lunch money, picture and banking money, roll call, notes from home, permissions, papers to pass out, and homework to check. I had so many little operations that required my attention that children didn't get to work until about 9:00 A.M. even though some of them arrived on the bus at 8:20. About 9:00 A.M. I'd announce, "All right, class, today we will. . . ." Work didn't begin until I started everyone out together. A terrible waste of time.

Now if I am teaching sixth period language arts, reading, or composition, students know that the minute they arrive in their seats they are to write or read for the first five to ten minutes of the period. Any time a student waits for me to start the class or the day is time wasted. In a class that meets daily it is possible to lose one full period a week just waiting for the teacher to start (five days times ten minutes equals one full period). In a month, a week of school is lost and in a year a full month and one half for that sixth-period class. For very young children it is possible to lose twenty minutes of instruction a day or two and a half hours a week or two days every month.

Usually there are items that need to be covered with the class at the start of the day. These can be listed on the board. Sometimes in a primary class I'll have the children work for the first forty minutes and then shift to an all-class meeting on the rug for the pledge of allegiance, sharing stories, and reviewing work and the schedule for the day.

ACTION:　　REDUCE TRANSITIONS AND INTERRUPTIONS.

Every time I must explain something new or make a transition from one learning experience to another, I interrupt work time. I want children to use time effectively, and they don't if I have to tell them what to do fifteen times a day. Some children finish early (the best student as well as the student who struggles most). Both need to know what to do when they finish or when a break or change of pace is needed in their work. Above all, I want to help children learn to sustain both reading and writing around questions of importance and interest for fifty to eighty minutes by the time they are in second grade. Keep track of the sustained learning opportunities your children have in one day. At the end of two different school days look over your plan and examine how time was actually used. Note the amount and frequency of the sustained work periods during which you did not interrupt with directions. Is it

- Five-minute learning stretches?
- Ten-minute?
- Fifteen-minute?
- Twenty-minute?

- Thirty-minute?
- Forty-minute?

Working with Chapters 4 and 5, try to find ways to help children have the sustained time they need to work.

Teachers throughout the world are faced with an ever-increasing number of interruptions. Here is a short list of some of the most frequent types I've observed in school classrooms:

- Announcements from the front office on the intercom.
- Notes from the front office announcing rescheduling of assemblies, video programs, visiting specialists in the arts, visits to the fire department, police department, and others.
- Specialists trying to rearrange the day.
- Specialists asking that certain children leave the room.
- Notes from parents containing special information for their children.
- Visitors to the classroom.
- Notes from other teachers in the school.
- Unscheduled evaluation sessions.
- Requests for paperwork you have forgotten to return to the office, such as supply lists, budget reports, committee reports, or checklists of faculty.
- Notes on children who are ill or held in the office for misbehavior or who arrive late on buses.
- Rescheduling of tests for groups and whole classrooms.

School parking lots are filled with many more cars than they were five or ten years ago. The number of administrators, teaching specialists, and visitors to schools has increased remarkably. With many more people vying for access to children, teachers, and classrooms, the number of interruptions was bound to rise. This can become a serious problem, especially where intercoms are overused. For many suburban communities, overscheduling, rescheduling, and interruptions have become a way of life. And the classroom suffers.

In this Action you will track two things for a week: instances of rescheduling and classroom interruptions. At the end of the week opposite each rescheduling and interruption you will put a + if the item had no effect on instruction, a 0 if you couldn't tell whether there was any effect, and a − if there was evidence of a negative effect. Make a simple list of the reschedulings and interruptions but be sure to provide ample room for additions you couldn't anticipate. Where possible, put down a time to indicate when the event occurred. If your children are old enough you may be able to enlist them in doing this record keeping.

Be prepared to share your list with the principal and with other teachers. In my first years as a school principal, I had no idea how many times I changed the teacher's day or the range and types of interruptions teachers had to face until one veteran teacher came to me and said, "I want you to see my week and how many times I've had to change my plans as well as how many times I was interrupted." First, I lived with the illusion that I was the only person who made changes in the teachers' schedule. Second, I didn't realize how many times my decisions indirectly forced teachers to change their daily plans. Teachers need to work with principals to review such data and their implications for the effective use of instructional time.

Our basic objective should be to provide as much straight, uninterrupted time as we can so that children will be able to pursue their reading, writing, and learning projects in an unbroken fashion. This means that we need to work hard in order to help children learn to use time well and in pursuit of realistic objectives. I examine the week to make sure that:

• Children read and write for a minimum of eighty to ninety minutes of sustained work daily.

• Children will not be interrupted by me or by the school any more than two or three times during the language-learning block.

If I am teaching in a department, straight time for student work is often more difficult to acquire. Nonetheless, I still want my students to have a minimum of thirty minutes of sustained work in a fifty-minute period with only two interruptions or a total of ten minutes of talk from me. (*Caution:* I use numbers here not to convey any exact amount but to show the relative proportion of independent student activity to teacher talk and interruption. On some days I may speak for twenty minutes and on other days students work the entire period and I merely move around the room conducting conferences.) Simply put, students should be doing large amounts of reading and writing without teacher interruption.

Principals often face an almost impossible task in organizing school schedules. The bus, cafeteria, visiting specialists, and additional demands from the community create problems that defy facile solutions. Teachers need to appreciate the enormous job scheduling entails. At the same time, they need to insist on as much straight teaching time as possible.

ACTION: FIND THE CHILDREN WHO DO NOT UNDERSTAND WHAT TO DO DURING READING AND WRITING.

In the best of classrooms there are children who do not understand the task at hand. They can spend hours—that turn into weeks—going through the motions of reading and writing, yet not truly catching on to what is expected. They are not difficult to spot: their output is low, and their papers are often messy and incomplete. During work time they wander, stare out the window, converse with other students, or recruit them into mischief. Enormous amounts of time are wasted by these children, and unfortunately, sometimes the waste can add up to a lifetime of schooling. In more cases than we realize, they simply do not know what to do.

In this Action you will review your understanding of problem children in two phases:

- Identify the children in your classroom who do not understand the immediate task at hand, whether it is what to do with their books and response letters or what to do with their writing.
- Identify the children in your classroom who do not understand what reading and writing are for, who simply cannot conceive of how reading and writing are relevant to their lives at that moment.

Task representation   Start with the three or four children in your room who waste the most time. Choose them because they are idle, fumbling with their work, or doing things not connected with reading and writing. First, ask about what they have done so far: How did they do it? What did they have in mind? If their paper is blank, take work out of their folders. Your objective is to establish a history to the current book or paper they are working on or to their writing folder.

Children who are wasting time are usually uncomfortable with an inquiry about their activities. You probably won't be comfortable either. When I think back to my teaching days, I remember well the children I used to glide by simply because I couldn't bear to look down at their blank or messy papers. These were the children who smiled deferentially, who were easily embarrassed, and who worked hard to go unnoticed. Their schemes usually worked: consciously, at least, I didn't notice them. I suspect that in a nine-month school year they wasted at least seven. With each succeeding year in school their ways of avoiding tasks and going unnoticed became more elaborate.

More obvious were those children who defied not only the assignment but literacy itself. Their schemes for effective defiance grew each year. They fought with their papers, me, other children, and the entire institution. Their bodies, minds, and mouths all moved at cross purposes to school activities or any work they had to do alone. I wrestled, fought, and pleaded with these children, but their papers remained as empty and scraggly as those of the children who tried to disappear. They were irritants who leaped across my mind before I fell asleep at night. Both groups wasted time.

An approach to the action The best approach is one of calm inquiry. I try to elicit an effective history of the child's previous activity, no matter how meager that past is. If the page is blank, I ask the child to take out his folder and review what he has done before. I want to point out to the child what he has tried to do in the past. Above all, I want to help him know what he *can* do. The more difficult the case, the harder I have to look: "I see that you have written about robots, a space story, and over here a piece about a rabbit you had. Tell me about your rabbit." I want the child to begin to hear his own voice actively using information. What he has written before is more real to him if it is expressed, however indirectly, in his own words.

Next, I want the child to discuss his current piece. Sometimes the new piece comes from something triggered in his folder. I spend a little time working from the folder, discuss current thoughts, and then quickly move to the new piece. Here is my conversation with Mark, a fifth grader:

DON: You are on a soccer team. Tell me about the team. How is the team doing? [*I ask this question based on what I already know about each child.*]

MARK: We've only won three games. We don't seem to be able to get anywhere. Some of the kids don't show up for practice.

DON: But you do.

MARK: Yeah, my dad says if you are going to play you have to stick to it.

DON: And you want to play.

MARK: Yeah, I sort of do, if we could only win.

DON: What position do you play?

MARK: I'm the goalie.

DON: Tell me about one you blocked in the last game.

MARK: There's this guy on the Hornets who really gets me. He's always bragging about how they'll cream us, especially him. Said he'd score four goals against us. They lead the league, and anyway, he comes in and it's just me and him, a breakaway they call it, and as usual my backs are upfield. He likes to blast it. And, like, I stand there helpless, only I'm not. Like I knew he'd kick it straight on and you have to watch their eyes. And his eyes said he'd drill it right at me. So I took a short step out toward him to make him get rid of it early. He kicked straight on like I said and it was an easy stop.

DON: Sometimes writers need to write almost anything just to get primed. But, in your case, you had a real story about the breakaway. I'd like you to write rapidly starting where you did with the kid from the Hornets and tell it in order from there. So, tell me your first line.

MARK: There's a creep on the Hornets.

DON: Got it. Now tell me a line for the ending.

MARK: He tried to spike it and I caught it.

Children like Mark, who are stuck or have lost their sense of what writing is for, are usually imprisoned by the present. The blank page confronts them; their sense of accomplishment is low and they experience the sense of loneliness that goes along with having no ideas to write about. My strategy is to work with such a child's past to help with the topic he may have in mind for the day; if the child has no topic then I will choose one I hope he can handle, discuss it, and then wait until the child can frame in a beginning and an ending to the piece before I move on. I don't want children like Mark to wait for two days before starting to write. I also work hard to show children what writing is for. When I return to Mark's seat I will respond to what his words have taught me. I will look especially for something in the text that he did not mention orally. I want him to know that his words connect.

Of the two general types of children I've mentioned, the child who tries to disappear and the active, openly hostile child, the former is the more difficult to help. Children like Mark reveal a voice when the discussion reaches into territory they know. But for the moment, these children have not connected literacy with their own important knowledge. Until Mark connects literacy with his own living and learning, his use of time will most likely remain tentative and inefficient. The way I use my time, therefore, is governed by my concern with helping Mark connect with a sense of what writing is for.

Angela is a child who doesn't want to be seen. Her dress, voice, and activities are directed away from herself. She rarely volunteers in class. She has one friend in the class with whom she speaks, a girl who has a similar need not to be noticed. Since print is a social medium, a means of communicating with ourselves and with other people, the challenge in trying to help a child like Angela is greater than with a child like Mark. I need to observe her quietly. "I see that you read your book this morning, Angela." Or "You have your paper out and you are getting ready to write. Right now you are probably wondering what to put down." I notice and I wait. I want to listen and then nudge gently. I approach her the same way I do Mark, discussing her previous pieces and pausing long enough for her responses, sometimes as long as twenty or thirty seconds. Children like Angela often feel as though the world is moving at high speed, that it makes no provision for children who need to pause in order to relax enough to find words in the midst of worry.

ACTION: RETHINK HOW CHILDREN USE THEIR TIME DURING READING.

The most common time waster in the field of reading is the traditional "reading hour." I am speaking of the "three group" approach to reading in which children are called in clusters to read from the appropriate book in a basal series. When they are not working in small reading groups they work on a series of skill sheets from workbooks and dittos. Time is wasted for these children because they spend so little time reading. It is well documented that children do straight reading for only four to six minutes in the common reading hour.

Children learn to read by reading. Children should read for thirty to forty minutes every day. Naturally, the amount of time will vary with age and children's experience in reading books. But there is no more efficient use of time than when children are "lost" in the books they love. Even the most seasoned and dedicated professional who has devoted a lifetime to work in skills has to recognize that a child reading nonstop for twenty minutes has done the following:

- Applied phonics.
- Worked to understand the relationship between the information at hand and the overall direction of book or story.
- Unlocked new words in context.
- Used picture cues.
- Reread to rethink meaning.

Teachers at Stratham Memorial School in New Hampshire let children read trade books as their regular reading diet. The books come from school and classroom libraries, home, friends, bookstores, anywhere they can get their hands on them. When children are allowed ample time to read, they read extensively and with purpose. They use their time well.

We discovered the same pattern in the teaching of writing. Children who wrote only one day a week disliked writing. Their avoidance strategies were legion. But allow children the opportunity to write four days in a row and they will complain when the teacher misses the fifth day. Children who wrote regularly used time well during the actual writing, but they wrote even better when they were challenged.

The child who reads in school reads at home. This is a wonderful use of time. I used to assign reading for homework, but the children read only a little at home on their own, and reluctantly under assignment. Nancie Atwell (1987) showed us that when her students read in school they read at home. Her reasoning was simple but correct. If children are in the middle of a good plot, they'll read at home without assignment. If a child already has begun reading about her project on squirrels in school, she'll have the momentum to continue to work at home. We have found the same to be true at Stratham Memorial School, where we are just completing our study of how children, teachers, and administrators changed what they valued about reading and writing over a three-year period. Children who read in school read at home and in abundance. Reading six books each month was not an unusual accomplishment for an average reader.

ACTION: MAKE THE SWITCH FROM BASALS TO TRADE BOOKS.

The term "basal" applies to commercially produced readers compiled by many authors working under a senior textbook editor to present reading skills systematically from kindergarten through the middle school years. "Trade" books are basically those books available in bookstores and libraries that are written by professional authors who simply present information or tell a story with no ulterior motive about teaching reading.

I have witnessed several ways of successfully moving from basals to trade books. One teacher had worked with basals for about twelve years; she liked their orderly, systematic approach. A cautious person, she decided to begin by allowing children to read trade books on Fridays. Her children were used to writing daily, exercising effective topic choice, and working with skills lessons, so the transition was an easy one: the children functioned as they had in writing. Within three weeks she had made the complete transition from basals, moving from one day to two days and then to five days of reading trade books. Her only condition was that children choose three types of books: an easy, a medium, and a challenge book. Some children chose all easy books, others books that were too difficult. All three types belong in a reader's diet. Sometimes the child was still unable to choose well. In this instance she would say, "This week you choose two books and I'll choose one."

Another teacher simply changed outright, saying to the children, "Today for reading I want you to choose a good book to read. I will be reading for a short time myself and then I will visit to see how you are doing." As in the first example, the children were used to daily writing and making effective choices. They made the change instantly.

Both teachers had to make adjustments. The children needed to respond to their books. They began by writing weekly letters to the teacher as well as to their classmates. Small groups met to review various authors and characters, and to read aloud and discuss the books they were reading. Children of all ability levels were able to make the switch easily. Their effective use of time changed dramatically. The minute they finished one book they simply started another. (See Graves 1990.)

ACTION: ABOLISH READING GROUPS.

Abolishing reading groups is more radical than the switch from basals to trade books, yet it will have the most positive effect of all on children's reading. It also saves time, especially for children who used to be in the lower group. Children who are reminded each day of their low-ability status by the teacher-sanctioned organization of the classroom waste time. They putter, avoid, and sense within themselves the hopelessness of achievement. Worse, they are cut off from the very children who may help them and to whom they have unique contributions of their own to make. Still worse, they do not read. Their skill sheets and ditto exercises keep them away from books. The children who most need to read have the least contact with books. Their time is wasted.

ACTION: FIND THE LIFELONG READERS AND WRITERS.

Until you give children extensive amounts of time to read, allow them to exercise effective choice in choosing their books, and change your approach to classroom grouping, you will find few lifelong readers and writers. When children have a choice and can exercise initiative, you will have a better chance of finding the children who will be actively literate for the rest of their lives. This Action helps you to identify children who will probably use reading and writing on their own as adults. It also pinpoints the main objectives of this book and the others in The Reading/Writing Teacher's Companion series. Look for children who demonstrate the following characteristics of the lifelong literate person:

- Chooses books independently and reads them without undue prodding.
- Responds to the text orally and in writing and in a manner that reflects the text's relevance to current living. ''The boy in this book went through the same things I did when I lost my dog.''
- Shares books with others. Knows how to talk about books and writing with other children.

- Uses reading and writing to learn. "Julia wanted to learn everything she could about beavers. She took two books out of the library, read selected portions, and used the information to write her piece."
- Knows what she wants to learn in order to be a better reader/writer. If I ask her what she needs to learn next, she knows with some degree of accuracy.
- Can state plans about what she wants to read and write next.
- When stuck on a book, word, or assignment, knows where to go for help.
- Understands the power of writing—that is, uses writing to affect the thinking of others and in places beyond the classroom.
- Can state how she best learns and can apply that knowledge to learning more from others and from the books she reads, and the pieces she writes.

We wish to find these children in order to assess the effectiveness of literacy in our classrooms (see Chapter 10 for more detailed information). At the same time, we know that enormous amounts of school time are wasted by children who see no relevance to their lives in the consumption and use of print. The problem will worsen as children advance in school unless we actively help them during their first years in school. Outlined here are some of the barriers to becoming lifelong readers and writers and some recommendations:

- Self-diagnosed poor reader/writer. These are the most difficult children to help. Furthermore, these children will waste the most time simply because they do not see the relevance of most tasks. These children often have a long history of remediation. They have been removed from the room for Chapter I help, work in the resource room, and clinical work with a variety of specialists. Worse, they have often had conflicting assistance because no one has consulted with them or their classroom teacher. Several years in the "low reading" group will also help to confirm their self-diagnosis.

- Lack of an effective audience. Reading and writing are social acts. A good proportion of their products are meant to be shared with others. If the classroom audience has learned how to help, the sense of relevance of these acts is increased.
- Lack of skills. Some children may want to read and write but lack the skills to acquire any kind of fluency. Work with sound/symbols and context clues or practice with invention in writing and with some of the conventions of reading and writing are sometimes needed. Rarely are skills deficiencies the sole reason that children do not learn to read or write. They must be seen in the context of the other issues listed here.
- A sense of a need to read and write. How often are the uses of reading and writing really needed? That is, are letters written to people who need information? Are reference sources read because people actually need the information? Review the chapters in this book "What Reading Does" and "What Writing Does."
- Lack of positive learning history. How well can children articulate what they *can* do? The poorer they are at learning, the more children need to know what they can do.
- Ability to make plans. Unless children know what they need to learn next in order to be better reader/writers, or what they will read/write next, there is little momentum to their learning. But plans for the future are often *preceded* by the ability to articulate what they already can do effectively in reading and writing.

- Lack of challenge. All children need a challenge that falls within the framework of their past experience and their potential ability. Challenges affirm that the children are learners. Children who do poorly are often aware that the "good learners" receive challenges, whereas those who struggle do not.
- Lack of demonstration. Children need to see how reading/writing fits into the teacher's life. They become apprentices to a professional who demonstrates the power of reading and writing in her own life. The teacher may also bring in people from the workaday world who share their sense of the place of reading and writing in their lives. Here, it is important that people from a wide variety of jobs, not all professional, be invited to the classroom.

FINAL REFLECTION   As a teacher, you know when a child's time is being wasted better than anyone else in your school. You also know which children are in danger of not becoming lifelong readers and writers. You have carefully considered which elements in the school curriculum need to be brought together in order to save time.

If you have followed the Actions in this chapter, you have gradually phased in a system that allows children greater independence: they know how to start the day on their own in reading and writing. Best of all, you have provided uninterrupted time for both reading and writing. The children can read and write for as long as an hour at a time and solve enough problems on their own to sustain their efforts.

So much of good teaching is demonstrating to children how you solve problems so they can see how to solve their own. You know that covering the curriculum and correcting papers do not show children how to learn. Your children will take their place in the society of the twenty-first century knowing how to help others help them when they encounter problems. They will be good teachers because they constantly practice with other children the very demonstrations you have used in class.

3

structure a literate classroom

It is often thought that, since literacy is such a natural act, a fully "natural" environment is needed. Not so. If the classroom is not carefully designed and structured and continually adapted to meet the shifting social and learning needs of the community, then children's natural urge to express themselves will be thwarted.

A natural environment would mean letting you and the children occupy a room where there was little definition to either territory or process. If I imagine a classroom in which a laissez-faire mood exists, I see the children reading and writing when they want, about what they want, and completing products as they please. They discuss the work of others, either punishing or applauding. A natural environment is an invitation to a junglelike existence in which children violate the territory and interests of others. A natural environment, without any structure, allows each child's notion of territory and ownership to compete for center stage. The richness of the many cultures and family traditions represented in the classroom is then lost.

Children come from a variety of home environments. Some are autocratic, others democratic, permissive, or interventionist. Some parents use physical punishment while others speak words that humiliate. In some homes, children see all property as held in common—what is in the house can be used in play—but severe punishment may be meted out in another household if certain objects are not held in esteem.

The most trying child in my classroom usually comes from a family in which there is a constant and unpredictable shift between punishment and praise, control and permissiveness. Children in these families cannot establish a rhythm in their emotions or in their day.

There may be even more radical differences in the use of time. Some children eat with the family while others pick up food as they wish; some eat fast food while others sit down to a well-prepared meal with carefully defined customs and table manners. Other children are simply hungry or severely undernourished. Many children arise at 5:30 A.M. with parents who leave for work at 6:30; others go to bed at midnight or whenever they feel tired; still others follow specified bedtimes that hardly vary by even fifteen minutes.

Each morning, children from all these backgrounds—which differ in family and ethnic customs, in their uses of space and time, in their patterns of negotiation, and in their understanding of the meaning of speech and print—enter the classroom. You prepare for their entrance with a predictable classroom, which encourages highly creative, unpredictable, and delightful expression to flourish.

In the short run, you could deal with this enormous range of differences by exercising total control of time and space in the classroom. The children could follow a tight regimen in which they function only at your direction and on your timetable. In this approach the room is predictable, and the children are secure in the knowledge that there is only one task: to please you and do as you wish. But they acquire very little learning about how to use space and time on their own or to negotiate with each other. Worse, they do not learn how to develop structures of their own.

Although there are those moments when I function autocratically ("The job will be done *now* and *this* way"), my preferred route to the development of an effective classroom is through a *cooperative* structuring of the basic phases of room operation. The children and I need to learn how to use time and space to make a room that fits the contours of our needs yet still allows us to function as a community.

I am committed to the belief that an essential achievement in any teacher's or child's survival tool kit is *learning how to become a community*. Communities function well when the members take on the many responsibilities involved and use them to learn from each other and to help each other learn. If writing and reading exist to help me communicate with myself and with others, I need an effective community that has learned to negotiate texts, time, and space in order to learn how to use writing and reading effectively.

Delegating responsibility is at the heart of the structured classroom. If I want children to be able to use time well, for example, they occasionally need to undertake projects that engage them for as long as several hours. If a child does not understand how the room works or that children take on many responsibilities in order to sustain it, then that kind of important learning will be lost (see Chapter 2). A structured room is also essential to my own attempt to provide a studiolike atmosphere. In a room where I want to demonstrate, conduct conferences, and convene small groups of children, I need a class that knows how to operate without my immediate attention.

When you delegate responsibility to children you share your power. You do this because you are confident in your own ability to learn and you know that children need to practice taking responsibility in order to become more proficient and powerful learners themselves. When you delegate responsibility you take the most fundamental step in establishing the structured classroom.

Leslie Funkhouser knows that children are perfectly capable of organizing and maintaining the two hundred or so books in their classroom library area. Each week someone is responsible for making sure that books are neatly back on the shelves in their proper classification and are maintained throughout the week. Shared responsibility contributes to a child's sense of independence, but it also sustains the underlying organization of the classroom as well. As the year progresses the children gain more and more experience in many of the twenty-three responsibilities she carefully delegates to them.

Leslie works at her personal organization and at identifying what she has to give away. "Let's see, what am I doing that the children ought to be able to handle?" Each year, as she learns more about delegating responsibility to children, she adds to her list of what children can handle. Many of us haven't yet learned what responsibility children can take on because we haven't fully learned how to delegate.

This chapter will deal with Actions that focus on the systematic delegation of responsibility to children. I want to review the process of delegation and the philosophy behind it. Delegation requires conscious decision making on the part of the teacher. It begins with the notion "I want children to need me *less* so that I can choose more effective moments for real teaching."

WHAT TO DELEGATE   Every class is different. Some get along better with each other than others and can negotiate territory and responsibilities more effectively. Some classes seem to learn to handle independence rapidly. Others are terrified at first; for them the responsibility is a chore, not an opportunity to help. This seems to be a greater problem as children grow older. Thus, "decentralization," or dividing up responsibility, is often much easier in kindergarten than it is in fifth grade. To a large degree I believe it is the fault of schools. We seem to be too effective in helping children to know what they cannot do to the point that they fear responsibility because it seems designed to display their incompetence.

In Leslie Funkhouser's second-grade classroom there are several types of responsibilities: room maintenance, interpersonal activities, and general self-directed classroom activities.

ACTION: PHASE IN RESPONSIBILITY FOR ROOM MAINTENANCE.

Most children can handle room maintenance activities from the very beginning of the year. Each week the jobs are rotated on the job chart with some overlap so that last week's person can help with the more difficult duties. These jobs take only a few minutes a day and contribute significantly to the understructure and predictability of the classroom. They also free you for the important work of class preparation and teaching.

- Weekly papers: Papers that are reviewed by the week are passed out by an individual child, who sorts them and delivers them to the children on Friday to go home.
- Library: Someone keeps the classroom library books in order for a week. If books are coded by type and go in certain bins or on certain shelves, then that person also double-checks the placement of the books.
- Messenger: This weekly task involves carrying notes to other teachers and the main office or handling any other type of communication.
- Milk tickets: Simpler to handle than hot lunch, this job requires only a minor amount of math. Rotates on a weekly basis.
- Boards: Caring for chalkboards is done at the end of each day if any need cleaning.
- Attendance: Daily attendance is handled in weekly shifts. A slip is sent to the office daily and is double-checked by the teacher, who lists absentees.
- Bulletin boards: The design and layout, as well as the actual mounting of materials on the bulletin board, is handled by a rotating committee of children.
- General room cleanliness: A weekly job in which two people see to the general order and cleanliness of the room. Messy desks and cubbies, stray papers, and other problems are observed and cared for as needed.

You will have your own kinds of responsibilities to delegate. Find out from other teachers what they delegate to their children; then find out how they helped children handle the responsibility on their own.

ACTION: PHASE IN INTERPERSONAL RESPONSIBILITIES.

Although mechanical tasks often demand interpersonal skills because children's work brings them in contact with one another, there are specific tasks that require personal negotiation and consultation. Children need practice in gathering information from other people and using it to help the entire class. These delegated responsibilities require you to do more demonstration and follow-up, and to enlist the help of children who are experienced in those areas you wish to delegate. Here are some of the responsibilities:

- Host or hostess: Children escort visitors and help them to understand how their classroom works. They must be up to date on room procedures, materials, and some of the reasons behind various areas and activities. This is a weekly assignment and begins in September.
- Visitor invitations: There are occasions when it would be helpful to invite various experts or parent helpers to the room. This person handles the letter or phone call to make the invitation. The precise details must be worked out with the child in advance.
- New children: If you know in advance that a new child will be joining your class, then a member of the class (preferably on the same bus as the new child) can be asked to get books and supplies for the child and introduce him to the principal and special teachers. She can also help him with class routines, describe classroom areas, and guide him in using materials for the first two days in the classroom. There are many times, of course, when the new child arrives without warning and the designated child must begin work on short notice. Although this job can be rotated, the first child to take on this assignment should be

the child you feel can handle it best. The experienced child can then help another child to take on the responsibility.

- Sharing in other rooms: It is often helpful for children to share their work in progress or final work with new audiences. One child organizes the sharing, working from a particular child's request, consulting with you and contacting other teachers. This responsibility begins later in the year.

- Scheduling conferences: This responsibility can be delegated later in the year when children are effectively helping each other and know each other's writing and reading, and the room structure is working well. One child queries other children in the room about their sense of when a group or individual conference will be helpful. This child schedules conferences for all the children for one week. Naturally there will be times when the teacher changes the requests, but our experience shows that children can handle the main part of the scheduling quite well.

You will discover many other responsibilities that children can assume, depending on the needs in your classroom and the growing ability of children to assume them. I find that it is best to have the more skilled children handle a new responsibility first, then serve as helpers for other children the succeeding week. In fact, children of all ability levels help others to fulfill their responsibilities throughout the year. When responsibilities are broadly based and the jobs become interchangeable, and children learn how the entire room works from the vantage point of one job, they learn the structure that helps them to work independently. They learn how to consult with others for help; they especially learn the skills other children possess; and they learn to negotiate and complete their regular daily tasks.

ACTION: REVIEW RESPONSIBILITIES EVERYONE HAS EACH DAY.

These are responsibilities everyone assumes from day to day. Here is a short list:

- Record-keeping folders and/or portfolios: All children maintain their folders and portfolios; for both their reading and writing they keep track of titles and dates started and finished. (See Chapter 10.)
- Library: No more than three children go to the library at any one time, but they can come and go all day long as their need for reading material and information requires. There are three spots on the chalkboard; a child may go only if there is an open spot.
- Conference preparation: Before a scheduled conference the child is prepared to speak about her writing piece or a book she is reading by stating: "This is what it is about, this is where I am in it, and these are the problems I am encountering or enjoyable things that strike me."

GETTING THE BUGS OUT In some cases, either the room as a whole or individual children are not ready for some responsibilities. When things don't work well, I consult the class about how we can make the room work better. In fact, on the first day of school when I begin to delegate tasks, I state how I hope our room might work: "This is our room and I expect us all to help it become a place where we work together to help us learn (and that includes me) and enjoy our time. That means that each of us has a responsibility to make it work; some jobs we will have every day; others I'll give to certain people each week starting right now."

I'll mention a few of the responsibilities I have in mind, then ask them to cite some they have been assigned in other classrooms. I want children to get used to being consulted on matters of room improvement. And I consult for ideas, not for "yes" or "no" answers, whether I am dealing with a text in reading and writing or classroom management. The children know that when I ask questions I don't have the answers in advance. These are the questions that give them experience in solving problems.

Another experienced teacher I know starts the year out by planning the actual room organization with the children. This means that when the children enter the class on the first day the room is barely set up. In fact, they proceed to take everything down and gradually reorganize it, rearranging furniture, setting up learning areas, developing classroom routines, and even working on a massive learning project that will bring the class together. It is almost as if the class were in a camp for the first two days, defining routines and responsibilities.

Here are seven common reasons why delegation and certain room structures don't work:

1. *Students lack understanding of what delegation is for.* They don't understand what they are doing and how it helps the community.
2. *The task has not been demonstrated properly.* Usually this means the teacher doesn't understand the full ramifications of the task she has given. The teacher needs to do careful analysis of what the task actually involves. Usually children can be of great help to each other in breaking the task down into proper steps.
3. *The teacher hovers.* Although some follow-up is needed, the teacher should observe from a distance. If I sense that a problem has occurred, I'll ask the child, "How is it going? How can that be solved? If you get stuck, whom can you ask for help?"
4. *Too many responsibilities are delegated too quickly.* I may have delegated more tasks than I can demonstrate properly or observe effectively. The key is to start them slowly and

systematically, so that children can successfully help each other if follow-up is needed.

5. *Choose the right child to start.* Some tasks are more complex than others. If I understand what the task involves, I'll know how to select the first child to assign it to. The more difficult ones I'll give to children who will know how to handle any inherent problems; after that they can teach it to others.

6. *Be organized yourself.* If my own life is disorganized, that disorganization spills over into the classroom. I do not see the problems within the room. I need to have predictable rhythms in my own life so that they may continue in the classroom. That means much planning throughout the rest of my life outside of the classroom.

7. *Know what responsibilities not to share.* So much of learning how to delegate responsibility is in knowing when *not* to. The teacher is still the person who must take a major share of the responsibility for a successful classroom. This means that the teacher will make many unilateral decisions that go unnoticed by the children. In addition, there are some decisions that need to be taken from children because circumstances demand it: safety is involved, or there is decision overload, or the child simply cannot understand what has been delegated. Children need to see the teacher decide under these circumstances. This is the safety net that enables them to learn how to handle responsibility comfortably. There are times when a child needs to be able to give responsibility *back* to the teacher. On some days, certain jobs may not be appropriate.

ACTION: HELP CHILDREN LEARN TO NEGOTIATE.

When many people share the same space from 8:30 A.M. until 3:00 P.M. and from early September until late June, they need to learn how to negotiate when human differences arise, as they are bound to do. When children have a choice and many different tasks to perform and a fair amount of freedom to move about in the room, then the ability to negotiate is essential. In a larger sense, the ability to examine an author's point of view in a text and understand many classmates' points of view is an essential component of the literate person. When I read and write I need a realistic sense of audience. The ability to negotiate helps that very important tool.

Even though limits on the number of children who can work at certain activities at any one time are sometimes necessary, exceptions constantly occur. Two children want the same book; a child wants to copy an illustration from another child's piece and the artist doesn't want to share it; still another child wants help but the potential helper is busy. Effective negotiation begins with a sincere wish to gather facts: blame is always set aside during negotiation. Show children how to negotiate by using the very issues that arise in class. For example, in a classroom where children are allowed to choose, two children have been arguing over a particular book. Both girls want the same book, and each feels justified in keeping it. They have brought the matter to the teacher.

HEIDI: Jennifer has the Ramona book and she won't give it back.

JENNIFER: I've been reading Beverly Cleary books and this is the next one I'm going to read and Heidi said I could have it next.

MRS. P.: Let's see if I have this straight. Heidi, you want the book and, Jennifer, you said this was the next one you were going to read and Heidi said you could have it next?

HEIDI: I did but I wasn't finished with it yet. I think I should be able to at least finish it.

JENNIFER: If she finishes it now I won't get it until next week sometime. She takes so long to finish books.

HEIDI: No I don't . . . and I won't with this one.

MRS. P.: When do you think you will finish, Heidi?

HEIDI: I'll finish in two more days—on Thursday.

MRS. P: Then Jennifer can have the book on Thursday afternoon, Heidi?

HEIDI: Yes.

MRS. P: What will you read in the meantime, Jennifer?

JENNIFER: I don't know [*sighs*].

MRS. P: It's hard to wait when there's a good book in the room. That's short notice for deciding on another one. Find another one now; or, you've also got the other two books you are reading to keep you busy until Thursday.

Jennifer's eagerness to read Beverly Cleary made her take a book that Heidi had technically given her permission to read. Heidi is a slower reader and Jennifer is impatient. But classroom guidelines hold that a person reading a book has first rights to finishing it. Both Jennifer and Mrs. P. knew the room guidelines hadn't been observed. Instead of accusing Jennifer of taking the book, Mrs. P. let the guidelines run their course through negotiation. She also recognized that Jennifer would have a problem in not getting the book she wanted. Two choices were open to Jennifer: she could pick another book or work on the two others she was already reading. Jennifer needed reminding that she already had a course of action.

This incident is an example of a teacher-selected negotiation. On occasion Mrs. P. will choose to participate in this way if she thinks a demonstration will help children learn how to handle problems. But her more common course of action is to say, "How are you going to handle this?" or "You know the room guidelines: you can handle this perfectly well."

FINAL REFLECTION Classrooms need careful structuring so that children can function more independently. Structure also helps to integrate the enormous range of differences among children in any classroom. Structure and responsibility must be carefully developed throughout the school year: what is possible in January may not be possible in September. You will find that you and the children grow in your ability to make the room function more effectively.

Providing structure and delegating responsibility are often effective for a host of reasons I have not mentioned in this chapter. Additional Actions in following chapters will focus on:

- Children's sense of potential (Chapter 8): When children feel that they can exercise talents that are important to them, they have a sense of place in the classroom. They are also much more secure in their ability to handle differences.
- Level of challenge (Chapter 9): Children who are challenged to go beyond their current performance can more easily understand the importance of structure in helping them realize their plans for learning more. It is equally important to have a collective level of challenge for the entire room. When children know that "together we have done these things this year," their general sense of an effective room structure and their ability to negotiate are aided. Negotiation for the good of the whole class is more easily conducted than mediation between two people who want something just for themselves.
- Quality of evaluation (Chapter 10): When children are able to make more effective qualitative judgments on their own, they are better able to evaluate how the structure of the room affects the quality of classroom functioning.

The highly structured classroom is a functional classroom. What is this for? and How does it enhance the quality of classroom living for learning? are questions you regularly ask of yourself and the children. The issue of function leads into the next two chapters: What can writing and reading do?

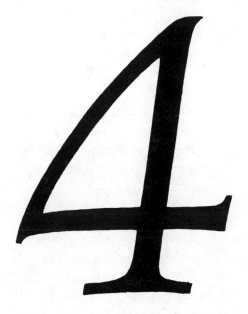

what writing does

Robbie was only six, but already he was an expert on pigs. His family raised them and Robbie regularly exhibited them as part of his 4H work at the county fair. He drew pigs, wrote about them, and delighted in being the resident class expert on the subject.

His teacher, Ms. Porter, worked hard to get him to include more information in his writing. The dialogue that follows demonstrates Robbie's understanding of writing in relation to speaking.

MS. P.: Robbie, I had no idea that a sow had so many piglets. Had you thought of putting that information in your piece?

ROBBIE: Why should I put it in? I just told you.

MS. P.: That's true, you just told me, but the other children aren't here. How can they know this information? Do you think it's important for them to understand how many piglets a sow might have?

ROBBIE: Sure, and if they want to know, they can ask and I'll tell 'em.

MS. P.: That's true too, Robbie. But what happens when you are absent like you were last Friday? Who can tell them then?

ROBBIE: Hmm. Hadn't thought of that. Guess I better put some of that in.

Both Robbie and his teacher are struggling with the meaning and place of writing. After the conference Ms. Porter said, "I was discovering what writing does right along with Robbie. It wasn't until my final question about how to deal with information when the author isn't present that I realized for myself one of the powerful features about writing."

Very young children find it difficult to conceive of moments when their writing is shared and they might not be present. This is one of the necessary transitions that everyone makes

47

when switching from oral to written discourse. To some degree I never get over the surprise I feel when someone comes to me and says, "I was reading your piece in *Language Arts*, and I enjoyed that part about the boy who was talking at the same time he was writing." The miracle of print never ceases to amaze me. It exists when we are not present; the words of my friends can be with me when I read in my living room in the evening although they are thousands of miles away. Writing helps me to discover things I didn't know about myself, or if I have a perplexing problem, I keep on writing until something emerges from the page.

Almost every writer, and every teacher who writes, knows these obvious facts about writing. But they are important enough for us to try to consciously help children understand the miracle of writing in greater detail. Writing has so often been taught with the dictum "Someday you'll need this; now get to work and write." When writing is taught well, we allow children to discover the place of writing in their lives right now, not at some abstract future time. We also explore and confirm together the relationship of writing to speaking and reading.

The Actions contained in this chapter are to be used in a timely fashion since they follow what is already evident to the class. For example, when children keep a chronicle of a series of events and that information is used again, point out or discuss what was unique about print in that case.

ACTION: HELP STUDENTS UNDERSTAND THE DURABLE POWER OF WRITING.

When Robbie spoke about pigs with his teacher, Ms. Porter, he treated his writing as he treated his speech. He didn't realize that others could obtain information from his words even though he was not present. Information was contained in the words that sat quietly on the paper. Unlike speech, where the transfer of information stops when the speaker stops talking, writing lasts.

Teachers like Ms. Porter help children understand the power of print because they call attention to what print can do. Try some of the following approaches to this Action to help your children extend their understanding of the uniqueness of writing:

- Keep writing folders. Children find that their information and knowledge visibly accumulates.
- Hold class discussions. What can writing do that speaking can't? What can speaking do that writing can't? that reading can't?
- Use pieces already written. Take out a piece a child has written several months or weeks before to look for information or a show of progress. Develop a sense of history.
- Keep records on the surveys, observation notes, and mathematical data children collect, then use the information again at another time to point out the lasting power of print.
- Read children's work when they are not present. Don't do it as a regular practice, but do it enough to help children see that their words work when they are not present. Discuss as a class the child's piece when she returns so that the child may understand that words exist when the writer is not present.
- Share children's published books. When other children check out a child's book and respond to it, the child can realize how his words can affect people at other places and times.

ACTION: HELP CHILDREN UNDERSTAND THAT INFORMATION CAN BE STORED THROUGH NOTETAKING.

Once completed, writing is seldom brought out again and used in the classroom. Other children may read a child's published book, and in this sense, the writing is used again and a notion of permanency is developed in both the writer and the reader. But the writing I am refering to here is writing containing information that is *needed at another place and time*. For example, if children are keeping daily records of the habits of young ducks, the conclusions they make about duck behavior at the end of the week require the use of all the information they have gathered.

Studies of young learners show that there are few events in their lives when they are required to go back and use previous information of any kind—reread a text, reexamine a math problem, or rethink a social problem in the classroom. The curriculum coverage demands of the future will provide no time for reflection or the reexamination of information gathered over time. Writing in journals, daily reflection, systematic record keeping, and interviews contribute to a different view of information than episodic reviews of skills or reading of short stories.

Children need to learn to acquire information from books and people. Most of their experience to date has been remembering information they hear from other children. If they are to remember more detailed information for use at another time, they need to take notes. Notetaking is a very demanding task because the listener/reader must abstract information on the spot. Notetaking from reading is less difficult than notetaking from speaking. Readers can at least go back and reread in order to abstract the essential information.

When children take notes while someone is speaking, they must know how to condense the nouns and verbs and abstract the ideas to get the essentials of the information down. Later, the reader can reconstitute the rest of the text. In this instance, the notes show us how a few words can stand for a much larger event.

Try some oral rehearsal with an overhead projector to help

children find out how to do this. Sometimes I bring in an object for them to interview me about, here a sixty-minute time clock.

DON: Ask me questions to find out all you can about this object.

CHILDREN: What is it?

DON: A timer. [*I write "Timer" on the overhead in one column.*]

CHILDREN: What do you use it for?

DON: I use it to time things. [*I write "Time things" on the board.*]

CHILDREN: What things do you time?

DON: When I get stuck I just write any old thing for ten minutes. I set this timer for ten minutes. It helps a lot. What words can I put over here that help you see what I was saying? [*I write "Ten minutes, get stuck, any old thing."*]

After pointing out these few words abstracted from our interview, I see if the children can remember what we were talking about. I might even bring these notes the next day to see if they help us remember. I'll be interested at all points to see who can remember what they stand for on the day they are used as well as on the day after. There are some children who can learn to do this as early as the second grade, and some who struggle to do it their freshman year in college. Abstracting, chunking information, writing précis, and recording data for later use are all tools that can probably be introduced much earlier in a child's school career than they are now, provided children have a sense that they will need the abstracted information at another place and time.

After children have learned to do some successful abstracting following me on the overhead or on experience chart paper, I'll ask them to try another interview with me, but this time they will write their own notes. We'll review what happened in the interview using their notes.

ACTION: HELP CHILDREN UNDERSTAND THAT WRITING INVOLVES
DISCOVERY.

It takes a while before a writer experiences the joy of discovery in writing. At first, young children believe words go directly from their heads to the page. When I ask a child with a partially filled page to tell me what will happen next, the child can tell me precisely what words will follow to the end of the piece. A short time later, I can almost match the words on the page with what the child told me since the correspondence is very close. But the child has experienced little surprise in the writing.

This particular phase of "in my head, then on the paper" doesn't last long if the child experiences a variety of audiences. Good audiences cause young writers to listen to their writing as they write. They develop a sense of options, of alternatives, to narrative, plot line, or the detailing of information. At first children are upset with the options: "I used to be able to write in third grade; now I can't." They confront options with a lack of decisiveness. In fact, options are opportunities for discovery. Problems with writing are also opportunities for discovery, the real joy of writing. It is essential that teachers treat the writer's problems as opportunities for discovery, one of the most important and sustaining aspects of writing. Professional writers write to discover; we need to recognize those opportunities when children can begin to listen to themselves, observe, and become conscious of new images.

I show the class in my own writing how I discover new things when I write. "Oh, I'd forgotten all about that. Didn't know it until I started writing this piece. That's what writing does; it helps you to remember, then to discover." Here is an example in which I talked aloud as I wrote on the overhead projector. (The written text is in italics.)

DON: I'm going to write now about my dog, Sadie. When we went on vacation it was as if she knew she was on vacation too. Ever think of a dog having a vacation? So, I'm going to write now, and when I do, I'm going to need to watch and listen. I'm going to look for pictures in my mind, and I'm going to listen for words that go with those pictures. I'll write the first line now. Watch.

During our long drive to the lake Sadie slept, curled up on the floor of the car.

DON: First thing you know I could hear a huffing, a kind of panting sound behind me. So, the thing I remember at this point is a sound. Then I turned to see her. What do you think I saw?

CHILDREN: The dog on the back seat.

DON: And I'll write that here, but I'm trying to remember just what she looked like. I'm trying to see. I remember she just looked funny. Ah, now I remember. Now I can see. I'll write that.

Then, as we approached the lake, she seemed to catch the scent of water or something. I remember a kind of sniffing, huffing sound behind me. I turned and looked. She had a happy dog look. Her ears were back and her eyes had that squinty look of satisfaction she gets when I'm about to give her supper. Every once in a while she'd toss her head and take a big sniff and look at me as if to say, "Almost there," and sit with her whole body awake for what was coming.

DON: I've written some things here so you can see the dog. Tell me what you see. Tell me what you'd like to see, what you wish I'd write here so you could see it.

CHILDREN: What color is she? We don't know what color she is. How big is she? Does she bite?

DON: Okay, I guess I could put some of that in. Where should I put it so it will help you?

CHILDREN: Right away, when she gets up on the seat.

DON: Okay. I'll try to help in this way. Let's see how it goes. [*Suggested additions are in roman.*]

During our long drive to the lake Sadie slept, curled up on the floor of the car. Sadie is a light tan, short-haired, gentle dog whose back is about as high as the chair you sit on to eat breakfast.

DON: Oops, I can see where that might confuse you. But let me ask you how high you think Sadie is. Let's see what picture I created in your head.

CHILD: She is this high [*indicates full height of the chair, including the top of the chair back*].

CHILD: No, he means the part you sit on.

DON: Well, you can't tell for sure, so I'm going to be more precise so you can tell more exactly how high she is. I'll write "as high as the chair seat you sit on to eat breakfast."

CHILD: Is that when she's standing, sitting, or running?

DON: Good question, and you still can't tell. I'll try again.

When she walks by, her back is as high as the chair seat you sit on to eat breakfast.

CHILD: Our chairs could be of different heights.

DON: True, but maybe most of your chairs are the same. But you are right, you might get a different picture of how high because your chair is different. It takes a little work for me to create a picture in my head that is close to the one in yours.

I'll write a little more so you can see Sadie. I can see her jump out of the car now, and I'll write what I see her do next. I'll make a picture.

I let her out of the car and she started running in circles like a football halfback on holiday. She's eight years old now but she ran

*and played like a little puppy. Her tongue seemed to hang out of
her mouth as if she couldn't control it and her eyes had that wild,
crazy look. Even her lips were pulled back as if she were smiling.
She finally stopped, panting furiously. I clapped my hands and
said, ''Go for it, Sadie,'' and she took off again, running and
zigzagging in wild circles around the trees, the picnic table, up
on to the porch, and down again.*

DON: I started at the beginning with the dog on the floor and
I could see her on the floor. My first memory was of her
snorting and sniffing in the back seat. I turned my head
and saw her there. I tried to remember what she looked
like and then I tried to paint with words, putting down the
details of what I saw, especially when she left the car and
started running. Most of all I remember her face with that
crazy, happy look that she was finally on vacation. Then
I saw her running. So, you can see my words follow what
I saw, but first I had to see. I want you to see what I did
and give you enough detail so you can make your own
picture. I think that's one of the miracles of writing: the
writer offers pictures to the reader so the reader can feel
what the writer did.

I try to show how writing also presents choices, then how new
discoveries come when I choose after I listen to my text and
try to visualize it. "What do you see?" I ask while talking aloud
to the class. That question or process shows that I listen to what
I have written.

ACTION: HAVE CHILDREN HELP EACH OTHER TO SEE.

Try this after you have composed with the children as I did on
the overhead projector. Ask the children to take out a piece of
writing they have already done. Have them choose a few lines
they can use as a base for further pictures. Or, they may wish
to create a few new lines on a different subject. Now, working

in teams of two, ask one child to read his piece aloud to his partner. The partner tells what pictures she saw or asks questions of the writer to bring out new pictures. The writer then goes to work to write about a few of the sentence pictures the partner brought out during the interview. This should take no longer than about ten minutes. In time, children ought to be able to initiate interviews with other children to help them see the pictures they need for their writing.

ACTION: LOOK FOR WRITING THAT CAN HELP OTHERS.

I write to make sense of something for myself. But if I am true to the subject and have listened carefully enough to my text, I will also make a contribution to others in the class. I want the children to realize that writing causes others to act, provides information for their own thinking and writing, and is a source of enjoyment as well as a medium that can trigger new thoughts, stories, and information in their classmates.

The children in Pat McLure's first-grade classroom at Mast Way School in Lee, New Hampshire, compile an information book on the hatching of their chicks each year. Other classrooms in the school find these records useful for their own work with chicks. She keeps the books from year to year, and in this way, the children can look for discoveries that may come one year but not the next.

Some children become known as "experts" on certain authors or subjects, such as prehistoric animals or unicorns. Their writing becomes a resource for others. I note this for children so that they can note this for themselves. "How did that piece help you? How did this book help you? Do you know of any people who might find this book useful?" I'll ask at the end of sharing session, thus enlarging their notion of what books can do. It isn't long before the children themselves begin to speak about how writing is useful to them.

Librarians can commission children to write books for the library on subjects that are in demand. These are books that are either in short supply or nonexistent. Children are capable of composing books in content areas for classroom and library distribution. High standards are set for such work, and these commissions help children to see how their work can inspire and influence others.

ACTION/REFLECTION: CONSIDER THE NEGATIVE AND THE POSITIVE FORCE OF WRITING.

Most people have vivid memories of learning to write. In 1978 I conducted a study for the Ford Foundation on the status of writing in the United States. We interviewed people from all walks of life, young and old, as well as professional writers. We asked them to share any memories they had that were connected with learning to write. Person after person recounted the painful or embarrassing experience of red-lining or trivial responses like "good," "poor," or "I liked your handling of this topic."

Later in the interview we asked, "Tell us about the teachers you had who saw something you wanted to say and helped you to say it." Most of the respondents couldn't cite anyone, some cited one person, and no one cited more than two. Few of the people we interviewed currently wrote unless writing was required in their occupation. These people had personal histories that not only made them feel inadequate as writers but prevented them from choosing writing as an important medium of thought and expression. Those who did choose to write, however, did so because of one teacher or one mentor outside of school. One good teacher, by helping the person through the writing process, contributed enormously to that person's long-standing development as a writer.

Reflect for a moment now and make up a list of memories associated with your own writing experiences. I'll do the reflection with you to show what I mean (see Figure 4–1), and

FIGURE 4–1   MEMORIES OF WRITING

Grade	Teacher	Writing in School	Writing at Home
1	Miss Jones		
2	Miss Jaegar		
3	Miss Wood	"Beavers" "Abraham Lincoln"	
4	Miss White Miss McGraw		
5	Miss Adams		
6	Miss Fortin		
7	Mrs. Thompson	Copying poems	West Point
8	Mrs. Kaftel		
9	Miss Hastings		Radio play
10	Mrs. Dower Ms. Fitch	John Keats Conservation	Jack London Diary
11	Miss Whitaker		Resolutions Diary church speech
12	?		College application

I'll comment on my list when I finish. Note that in the first column I list the grade, then the teacher's name, and then any memory. I also have a column on the right for any memory of writing outside of school. I'll put down a few words as a memory device for later comment.

As I review my writing history I am struck by how few memories I have from my elementary school days. I remember two pieces from third grade, but that may be because my mother kept them. Poor handwriting is my strongest memory of those years. The sighs of my teachers are a more difficult memory than their overt criticism.

In seventh grade, Albie Underwood and I decided to write a book outside of school. Inspired by a series of books we read about West Point, the beginning of World War II, and an urge to make money on a best-seller, we started our book. By Chapter 3 we ran out of gas, but that writing stands as the most significant of my first nine years in school.

In tenth grade, Mrs. Florence Dower, who was the first and only teacher to do so, responded to our writing in draft. She read our work, sensed our dreams, and helped us to rewrite until we began to realize them. I had to wait twenty-nine years to meet Donald Murray during my first year as professor at the University of New Hampshire before I received that same kind of help again. Make no mistake, many others have helped along the way, but there is something unique about the person who communicates a sense of potential to a writer and then actually helps the writer with tough questions and advice along the way.

For the longest time, the term *writing* meant handwriting. That shades my strongest recollections of writing from my elementary years. I hated to write because the teacher's first response was, "Donald, copy this over. You have written this carelessly. Try harder." My second and third attempts were never much better than my first. In desperation I switched to printing when I entered junior high.

As you look over your own profile, consider these points:

- Your most positive memory of learning to write. What did the teacher do to help you?
- Your most negative memory of learning to write. How did the teacher contribute to this unhappy memory?
- What role did problems with handwriting, spelling, punctuation, or grammar play in shaping your self-concept as a writer?
- How much do you use writing today as a means of personal expression? How much does your personal history contribute to your use or nonuse of writing?

You may want to consider an Action with children that reviews their brief personal histories as writers. What has helped them along the way? What writing is most memorable to them? Have they written some pieces from which they learned more than they did from others? What aspects of their writing histories do they wish to improve?

Some children find it painful to consider these memories, especially if they seem imperfect or punitive. Children who have spent more time in school and who can recall some difficult moments in writing often have negative views of writing and its accumulation. Linda Rief (1984) studied middle school students' understanding of audience in relation to what they did with their folder papers and discovered three distinct groups.

She was disturbed to find that the folders of her struggling students were empty. She knew they had been writing, but she couldn't find any of their papers. "I lost it . . . it was crummy; I threw it away. . . . I don't know." Since her study was on audience, she discovered that children in this category wrote only for her, the teacher. For these children writing was an assignment for the teacher that only brought out their personal imperfections. In their estimation, the accumulation of writing in a folder was an accumulation of personal failure.

The second group kept only their good papers and threw away the ones they didn't like, yet there were glimmers of a sense of audience emerging. Most still wrote for the teacher, but most could also cite one or two other people who might be interested in reading their papers.

The third group kept everything they wrote in their folders. In fact, most had kept papers from grade one. Their understanding of audience was extensive and diversified: they could cite many people who would read their papers. Their sense of personal history and accomplishment was strong. Furthermore, if asked about their future writing plans, they could supply a long list of possible topics. Their rich, confident writing history contributed to their excitement about new plans and topics.

Through her study, Rief realized the importance of audience and the conscious development of a personal history. Many of her students changed and folders began to bulge, but because the students were older and at the middle-school level, the task was much more difficult than with first graders. It is rare when first-grade teachers cite the problem of empty writing folders.

FINAL REFLECTION   Writing is one of the most concrete proofs that someone exists. Watch the fascination of young children as they view their squiggles and drawings on paper: "I made that mark. I exist" is the message that spreads across their faces. An accumulation of writing in a folder collected over a year's time or longer is further evidence of existence.

In a time of uprootedness within families and communities, where there is little concrete evidence of our own creations, a folder of writing—a collection of your own expression and ideas—becomes a baseline for personal reference.

"History" begins the moment I put a word on paper. The

words that tell about a personal experience or express an opinion about the food in the cafeteria are old the second they hit the page. But a rich history of lived experience—a sense of crafting through writing, of creating something that is shared with classmates—provides a launching pad for future thought. It gives a writer confidence that plans that have worked in the past can work in the future.

It is important that the children we teach have a sense of what writing can do. It is just as important that *we* have a sense of what writing can do. The word I write on the page creates a picture from my own past. It can be a hook that retrieves a long string of memories that add up to a narrative about personal experience, or a red flag that carries me into a testy essay.

Writing helps me to transcend myself in space and time. When I reread a piece I wrote months ago, I witness how I have changed since then; or I may reach into a chronicle I wrote many years ago to relive that day or retrieve information from it. These are the miracles of writing. When I write something, it may help a teacher across the hall or family members in another town, all because of the permanency of print. We can relive a memory or treasure the words of a friend.

The Actions in this chapter are meant to be used not as a unit or in sequence, but as reminders of what writing can do. Use them when the experience is evident to the entire class. For example, when a child refers to a piece written several months before, lead the class to see how, through writing, an experience has been frozen to be reexperienced at another place and time.

what reading does

I was six years old when my mother read my brother and me a story about a grandfather who built his grandsons a tree house in the biggest tree in the barnyard. That's my first recollection of a book that made me want my life to mirror what I heard in words and saw in pictures. I remember going to my grandfather and asking if he would build us a house like the one in the book. I don't remember what he said, but I don't think he built us a house in his barnyard.

In second grade I read a child's version of *Robinson Crusoe*. I went down to the Hudson River palisades to try to build a hut like Crusoe's surrounded by a fence like the one I saw in the illustrations. I wanted to relive the feelings I had experienced in reading the book. In fourth grade my dad gave me *Don Fendler: Lost on a Mountain in Maine*, a true story about a tenderfoot scout who survived fourteen days after he got lost on Mount Katahdin in Maine. I walked through the woods near my home pretending to be lost, trying to judge which direction was north and which south, keeping a cool head, and looking for edibles in the "forest."

Books do that for me. They move me to try new things, take on new lives through biography and autobiography, travel back in history or to a far-off place, or become a detective and solve a complex crime.

I am always struck by the power of words to evoke images. I was writing a poem the other day in which a caisson appeared. Instantly I saw a flag-draped caisson coming down Pennsylvania avenue carrying the body of John F. Kennedy. It was November and men were marching, stiff and respectful. I could hear the muffle of drums with their restrained, stately beat. One word—caisson—did all that. A miracle.

If I like the miracle I can revisit the scene and read about it all over again. There are some books I read again and again. *War and Peace* and *Anna Karenina* are two of them. I first read them in college and as I reread them periodically it is one way

I keep track of my own thinking. The words stay the same but I change. When I read, I circle myself nodding approvingly: "Ah, there's a good change" or negatively: "Oh dear, same old person; after all my attempts to be different my thinking has barely shifted."

My experience is not unique. Very young children produce the same images. Ruth Hubbard (1985, pp. 155–56) shares an observation she made at the end of a year studying children in Pat McLure's first-grade classroom: their discussions contain such a range of understanding about books and their purposes, as well as the images that books and print evoke. Here Pat had just finished reading *Charlotte's Web* by E. B. White:

The book talk began immediately. Barry cheered, "I love E. B. White's books!"

"And look," Roger commented. "The pictures are by Garth Williams—that's the same guy who did The Chick Story.*"*

After Pat read the day's chapter to her transfixed audience, Tara began the discussion.

"I saw the movie and the beginning was real different. There wasn't the wet grass . . . or the sneakers. And her brother carried a frog instead of a wooden gun."

Barry was still thinking about the illustrations. "I think the background looks like Stuart Little. *Did Garth Williams illustrate that too?"*

Dwayne focused more on the content. "That runt pig reminded me of Clifford. *He was the runt too."*

"Our cat was the runt," Roger added. "Now it's the biggest."

The children's responses draw on many images as they weave back and forth between personal experience, the words of E. B. White, and other books they have read. They are not trying to impress anyone with their book knowledge. Rather, they are so used to letting their image and story making run free that everything is grist for their thinking mills.

The children are doing many kinds of reading in this sharing session on *Charlotte's Web*. They read the story by composing their own images from the text Pat McLure has read aloud, they compose from the statements of their friends, and they do instant "rereads" of other books as conversation evokes images and storylines. That is the literate life, which involves constant reading of the world around us. And the world includes trees, friends, automobiles, towns, animals, and on and on. We try to read what is happening in our world, and the text on the page is but one part of the reading. Thus, the reading teacher teaches children how to read the world, and the book is but one small part of that world. Any notion of reading that does not try simultaneously to understand a world text—or a human text—and a written text misses the point of what reading and thinking are for.

WHAT READING DOES | We are often unaware of what reading does. We simply read. We are immersed in a world of print. Drive down the highway, walk through a shopping plaza, or look across the room where you are now seated. Print is never far away. It affects us even though most of the time we are unaware of its presence. This chapter seeks to help us as professionals to be aware of the effect of reading in our lives. Then we will take these insights and help children to do the same, to discover the power of print for themselves.

All reading is a kind of history. If there is print on the page, then someone at another place in time wrote it; the writing occurred before the reader picked up the paper. Reading with this sense of history affects us. We can enlarge on it in many ways:

- *Reading parallels our own experience.* If I experience the death of a friend, I can read about other deaths in order to understand and circle my own experience. If I play baseball

I can read sports stories in order to experience the same excitement I know through the story of another athlete. There is hardly a human experience that has not been written about. Yet even though these life events parallel mine, I know that my own is unique. I see the uniqueness of my own experience by recognizing how it is different from that of another person in what I read.

- *Reading extends our own experience.* Reading helps me to visit places before I travel or move back in time to other eras and cultures. I read *War and Peace* and I travel back to Napoleon's invasion of Russia, where I experience the philosophical struggles of Pierre over the ethics of war, the death of Bolkonsky, the love of Natasha. I live the lives of others but I live my own at the same time.

- *Reading helps us to understand people.* As I read autobiography and biography I review the full lives of other people and my own in parallel. Books allow me to see the long-term consequences of early decisions. I participate in the dilemmas of businesspeople, presidents, athletes, writers, and generals.

- *Reading provides storehouses of information.* Most of the time I can't talk directly to people ''in the know'' about a particular subject. When I want detailed street information about museums and restaurants in New York, I cross the room to pick up the *Blue Guide to New York*. The same shelf contains *The Complete Bicycle Fitness Book*, *AMC White Mountain Guide*, and *How to Know the Ferns*. These are all areas of personal interest about which my books provide the specialized information I need. I am not smart enough to know all that I want to know about these fields. The books wait to help me.

I have long been interested in the Soviet Union. Another shelf contains Russian literature, books on recent Soviet policy, and biographies of leading Soviet novelists and poets—my storehouse for easy access.

- *Reading provides relief and escape.* There are many times when I just want to be immersed in a book, to solve a murder mystery or fight in World War II. My reading is simply a means of leaving this world for another one. I have my escape shelf of adventure books and detective novels by Sue Grafton, John MacDonald, Robert Parker, and Nicholas Katzenbach.

- *Reading provides a taste for language.* Sometimes I read to taste the language of my favorite writers or poets. I remember a particularly difficult personal experience. I was depressed, and I went to my shelf of poets. For some reason, that night I picked up a collection of poems by Ted Kooser, whom I had first gotten to know through another collection of poems by Robert Wallace. I read one poem aloud, then the entire book. Three hours later I had read all of Kooser's poetry aloud. Kooser had taken me through my hour of crisis. For some reason Kooser's tone and subject matter, the agrarian feel of his language and the land he knew in Nebraska were close to my own feeling of barrenness. Lewis Thomas and Richard Selzer, both physicians, use language in a way that makes me want to read them aloud, to feel the presence of the author writing about subjects close to my own heart. Some of the other poets on my shelf are: Mekeel McBride, Charles Simic, Eamon Grennan, Richard Wilbur, Robert Frost, Marge Piercy, Sharon Olds, Anne Sexton, Donald Hall, Walt Whitman, Peter Meinke, William Carlos Williams, Dylan Thomas, William Stafford, and Ezra Pound. Some nights when I feel my mood waver, I grab a volume and just read aloud, waiting for the tones and senses to be right. I'm in a tasting mood.

• *Reading moves us to act.* When I was much younger, books moved me to immediate action. A reading of Robinson Crusoe led me straight out the door to build a hut on the New Jersey palisades. My responses are more cumulative and subtle now. Still, two weeks ago a Chinese student, Xiao Ming Li, gave me a copy of *The Mending of the Sky and Other Chinese Myths*, which she had translated into English. The simple yet profound stories triggered a line of poetry in my mind that made me drop the book and jot down the line before it evaporated. In the same way, *In Search of Excellence* (Peters and Waterman 1982) along with *Reinventing the Corporation* (Naisbitt and Aburdene 1985) brought to my speaking the immediacy of the need to decentralize and humanize administrations in the public schools.

These are only a few of the reasons why people read, or what books do for us. There are many more. How we use these categories is even more idiosyncratic; your escape will have entirely different routes and tastes. But you will escape. Still, we, along with the children, need to be more aware of what reading does for us, of what reading is for. The Actions in this chapter are directed to that end.

The Actions in this chapter are a bit different from those in other chapters of the book. When I help children understand what reading does, it is more of a joint activity than a directed kind of lesson. When a child expresses some emotional reaction to a book, for example, that is a timely moment to point out what reading does. Or, I may lead children into a situation in which the effects of reading can be seen more clearly. The following are general situations that help us understand more clearly what reading does:

• My own sharing of what I have learned about reading and what it does. This comes from sharing my own reading.

  • Interviews with adults and others about the place and function of reading in their lives.
  • The children's own discovery of what reading does as they read for themselves.

ACTION: TAKE A SMALL SECTION OF TEXT AND RECORD WHAT WENT THROUGH YOUR MIND WHILE YOU WERE READING IT.

Even a short section of text will contain many of the ingredients that strike us when we read other texts. I'll choose two very different texts to show what I mean. The texts I choose must be ones I have never read before. I'll pick up a book I bought yesterday at the Library of Congress in Washington, *The Human Experience: Contemporary American and Soviet Fiction and Poetry* (1989). I thumb through the pages and randomly select Boris Yekimov's short story "A Greeting from Afar." I will take the first three paragraphs from the story and, after typing them here on my computer, write what went through my head as I was doing that:

Bread wasn't delivered to the village everyday. So people stocked up on it: extra for themselves, and for their privately owned cattle when they were short of grain in their storage bins. On delivery days, people came early to avoid being last in line at the store and having to plead for leftovers. They sat around the entrance, the women with their knitting, discussing the village news and everything else.

A picture came immediately. A babushka in a kind of kitchen with a place where she kept bread, a kind of cupboard. She has a round loaf of hard bread and she is carving it. Out the window to her left is a field with cows in it and I wonder immediately on top of that picture, "How on earth could they ever maintain cattle with what little bread they've got to eat?" My mind wanders farther. Sounds like this is just

Now they were talking about Manya Kharitonova. Her sons had come for Manya and her husband the previous autumn, and taken them to live in the central settlement of the large collective farm, which included several scattered villages.

"I look around the bus station, and there's Manya. 'Hello, how are you!' And we chatted about this and that," recounted Arkhip, a lively, garrulous old man. Practically every week he was at the bus station, going off somewhere, on business or not, to Uryupinsk, sometimes even to the city, to visit relatives. "I say to her, 'I'm hurrying home to my old lady. The gardens are all in bloom now in the village. It's really beautiful!' And she, would you believe it, started to cry. 'I'll never see my village again,' she says. 'They've taken me off to some kind of barren steppe: not a garden, not a bus,' tears running right down here." Arkhip pointed with his nicotine-stained fingernail.

after the war was over and people had so little.

Soon there is old Manya in the picture and she looks like the woman in the first scene who had to share her bread with the cattle. I have a more complete picture of her now. Layers of clothing to keep her warm. They are tattered and worn so that any holes will be covered by the underlayers. She is stout with a broad forehead and a kind of mole to the left of her nose. She does not smile. Her eyes are grey, her cheeks puffy.

Arkhip wears a little black captain's hat, like those Russian peasants wear. He is fully bearded; the beard is white, accentuating his blue, dancing eyes. He is short and thin, smaller than Manya. Now maybe I have to change my picture, because if he was off traveling perhaps he has a different look, a slightly more businesslike look. But he is from the collective and therefore more of a farmer, a businessman farmer, and therefore my revision maybe *means he has more polished boots. The two of them meet in the bus station, a station with broad benches, crowded with people dressed in peasant costume. If Manya cries, I wonder why she is there. I want to know more about her displacement, the cause of her unhappiness. Pictures, then questions that go with the incomplete data I see and hear in the pictures. I am left with unhappy Manya and puzzled Arkhip. There is the sound of quiet sobbing and her voice stammering out the reasons for her unhappiness. Her arms wave slightly as she indicates that what she wants is not present.*

Most of what I saw was not in the author's description. But this is just the beginning of the story, and I work a little harder at the beginning to see and hear what is going on. I suspect, too, that what I have shared here in my written account is a little more detailed than the images and sounds in my mind. The questions that arise from what I see, however, are real and common in my reading. The author sows those questions so that I might read ahead to reap the harvest of the full story. The questions, triggered by the incomplete images, are what makes for good narrative and good reading.

I'll try one more passage from a very different kind of text to see what happens when I read. The following is the lead to a piece in *Phi Delta Kappan* (November 1988) by Joan First. The article was given to me by Debra Menkart, a friend from Washington, D.C., where we are working together on a project to help recent emigré Salvadoran children. The author's text is in the left column with the right column containing what the reading does to me:

Rosario Anaya, a member of the board of the San Francisco Unified Schools, has strong opinions about the American response to the challenge of educating immigrant students. "While we talk about democracy and equal opportunity," Anaya says, "in reality many of our students are barely given a chance to get out of the gate. We resist meeting immigrant children even halfway. The basic question is not how we teach these children, but whether we really want to."

Extensive immigration to the U. S. during the last 15 years has resulted in historic levels of enrollment of immigrant students in public schools. These new arrivals—largely from Asia, Latin America, and the Caribbean—are a vital resource for this country's

I see a young Hispanic woman, energetic, caring, leaning into her words. She is in an office, perhaps City Hall, high on a San Francisco hill. I don't know where City Hall is, but I know enough of San Francisco to decide she is up there; I can see the bay off to my right and the Golden Gate bridge off in the foggy background. She speaks, but when she speaks I also see Debra, the person who gave me the article, standing nearby. Debra will want to know my reaction to this piece. Through the author's words I see the same children from El Salvador I worked with in Washington last Friday. Their faces are eager to learn, but I am aware that the resources to help them are so limited. I refer to human resources, unprepared human resources, to extend future. But their extraordinary cultural diversity and unique backgrounds present difficult challenges that must be met if this promise is to be fully realized.

their eager yearnings for an education. Oh, how big we are with words in this country, political words that speak of bringing in the hungry and needy, saving the children from Vietnam and giving them a start. I am angry. These words make me bite off the words inside. Immediately I think of all our preparations for war and the Russian challenge to disarm and get on with other things. I feel selfish and angry with myself that I am not more active in campaigning for more resources for these children. I try to help children but my own response is as pitiful as my government's. President Bush stresses that local businesses and governments should take responsibility for easing this situation. We cannot look to Washington for full resources, but we need some help, some incentive, so that if we start our work will go forward. I have a heavy feeling about this problem, which is so enormous.

I am surprised that even in a piece of exposition I must start with an image. I must see where something takes place. I find that in conversing with someone I have met for the first time, I want to find out where they are from in order to picture their state, town, and home. I work for a picture, a context to put them in, and then our conversation goes on. I am surprised that Debra is there listening to my thoughts as I read. I find that people who give me things to read are often in my mind with the author of the piece when I read. The article made me angry and eager to act—now. Those Salvadoran children are waiting for me personally. Yes, it is personal, not unlike my days in fourth grade when I ran to the hills after school to "rediscover" America like the explorers did. I want to do something. Reading in this instance becomes a personal transaction between myself and the author.

For this Action choose passages from two entirely different types of text to see what goes through your mind. The underlying question is "How does reading affect you?" Reading is such an individual act that you will not have the same responses that I did when I read. You may not create pictures at all, and if you do, your pictures will be different. You bring entirely different experiences to the page. Still, this exercise will make you more aware of what reading does to you as you read.

Sometimes it's possible to ask children about what happens when they read. I've found that children may be able to respond if you phrase the question this way: "You've just read this part of the story. Do you remember what was going on inside your head when you were reading it?" I don't suggest what might be in their heads; I just wait for what they say. After they have spoken I may suggest some of the following: "Did anyone see any pictures in their head when they read? . . . hear anything? . . . feel anything inside them? . . . want to do something?"

ACTION: HELP CHILDREN SEE THAT BOOKS CAN LEAD THEM INTO VICARIOUS EXPERIENCES.

This Action is designed to help children become conscious of what books do through characters. Reading fiction carries children into the lives of the characters they read about. A child reads *Henry Huggins* by Beverly Cleary and experiences what it means to have a dog of one's own. Another child reads a series of Nancy Drew books and travels the more formulaic road to solving mysteries.

Help children to realize when they are following characters or are inside them trying on their personalities. I do this just after children share their books. It is natural for children to focus on the action of the characters: "He won the game. . . . He flew into outer space. . . . She tricked them and got them to show her where the jewels were hidden." Vicarious reading begins this way. Becoming the character in a book is an important part of finding out what reading does.

I am not much different from the children when I read my Travis McGee books by John MacDonald. Most of the time I ride McGee's back, cruising in his boat, the *Busted Flush*, driving a fist into the villain's stomach, or sprinting for cover under gunfire. But there are times when McGee launches into a discussion with his brilliant friend and economist, Meyer, that I crawl inside to try on the mind of my character as he discusses the latest issues in the economy or the ecology of Florida's swamp land.

Help children to see if they are following or crawling inside their characters. This is not a directed lesson but one that occurs after children have finished reading their books and group discussion leads into impressions of character:

- How did you feel when he fell off the horse? What made you feel that way? Show me the words where that happened.
- Were there times when you felt especially "there" during the reading of your book, as if you could see and hear

everything? As if you were inside the character? Tell me about it. Isn't it amazing that books can create pictures in your head? Just those words on the page?

ACTION: HELP CHILDREN BECOME KNOWLEDGEABLE ABOUT CHARACTERS THEY MIGHT LIKE TO BECOME.

When discussions focus on characters, children in the share groups can decide if they wish to become that kind of character. Try keeping a list on the board of favorite characters from book discussions or have children develop notebooks or a wall mural that shows characters through quotes or drawings portraying them as the children imagine them.

A fourth-grade teacher I know has a day when children become their favorite characters. Some dress up, but others simply act like the characters they imagine from their reading. The children try to guess which characters their classmates represent.

ACTION: HELP CHILDREN LEARN WHICH BOOKS PORTRAY LIFELIKE SITUATIONS THAT PARALLEL THEIR OWN EXPERIENCE OR INTERESTS.

Children can make lists of the human situations they encounter in their books that may be useful to classmates. Some of the situations that interest children are the following:

- Growing up, early adolescence.
- Death of a pet, parent, or relative.
- Divorce.
- Sports loss or victory.
- Dealing with a handicap.
- Driving a car.
- Severe illness.
- Physical bullying.
- Drug problems.

- Breakup with a friend.
- Misunderstandings with parents.
- Taking risks.
- Winning a prize or achieving a goal.

The list of human situations that children will find in books is endless. The point of this Action is to let children know that reading can do this.

ACTION: DEVELOP THE NOTION THAT BOOKS BRING PEOPLE TOGETHER
AND ESTABLISH COMMUNITIES.

I like to read aloud. I like to share the books I read alone by reading aloud to the entire class. I prepare for my reading by actually reading aloud at home, tasting and feeling the words in preparation for sharing them later with the children. I experience in private what I will do in public with the class.

When books are read aloud to children they experience the excitement of their friends in the story during suspenseful moments. They know the full range of joy, laughter, and sorrow as they hear together the story of Fern, Charlotte, Wilbur, and Templeton in *Charlotte's Web* by E. B. White (1952). As I read the children compose their own images, but the feelings they know together create a literate bond that is unique in human existence.

After a group seems to have sensed together the joy and emotional depth of hearing books read aloud, I call their attention to yet another instance of what books can do. I may ask a few questions like these, which lead to a sense of common experience:

- What were some of the feelings you had during the scene when Fern thought she was going to lose Wilbur?
- What pictures did you have in your mind?

These questions are not designed to be a quiz as much as to help the children see that reading aloud produces shared emotional experiences and possibly a few images in common from the text.

Reading is a social event. Even when I read alone I meet the many other sides of myself. I meet the wanderer who wants to be alone in the woods to view his birds, ferns, trees, and mountains. I meet the person who wants to be part of history, an executive perhaps, who makes decisions affecting monetary policy.

Many of my books I share with others. Our doctoral program in reading and writing at the University of New Hampshire seems to attract book pushers, both faculty and student. We read all kinds of books with a view to moving them on to the next reader. A sense of the next reader emerges from the text as we read, until finally we can say as we finish, "Here is just the book for you."

In our most recent study at Stratham Memorial School in Stratham, New Hampshire, the entire school, teachers and children, wrote weekly letters back and forth about their reading. The letters in most instances were natural conversations about books. Children wrote to teachers and to other children. They wrote back. The result: an unusual community within the classroom and the entire school. An example of an exchange between a student and a teacher follows. (See also Graves 1989, Chapter 4.) The following two entries give an idea of the tone and content of the letters. The first is from a fourth grader, the second, a sixth grader:

Dear Mrs. Herdecker,

Doggie falls into the water. He learns how to swim. It's weird because reading about pigs never was so good since Charlotte's Web. *I like it because I like animals that are like people. Like books by Thornton Burgess. The animals act like people. They talk, they wear clothes except in this book they don't wear clothes. This book they just talk to each other like Felicity the duck talks to Doggie.*

The pigs like Barly love, Mrs. Gobblespud, Mrs. Swiller, Mrs. Troughlicker, Mrs. Grubguzzle, Mrs. Maizemunch, and Doggie dogfoot. And the Squire. Those are all the pig characters.

from Jared

Dear Jared,

Your journal entry is super. It was wonderful for you to compare the animal stories of Thornton Burgess.

I had a feeling you liked animals. I can tell from your writing and reading.

Do you think animals can really talk to each other?

Love,
Mrs. Herdecker

Joshua Davidson   *2/1*

One Eyed Cat
Paula Fox

No. 3, Vol. 3

Dear Mr. N.

I'll start off as always by answering your letter. I sort of see what you mean. And I see how the clues make sense.

*Well, **One Eyed Cat** was kinda boring. Before you read the book the plot's given away. Not any action. Nothing really happens. Enough of this!*

I'm reading another Drew book. I can't help it. Jess buys more and I can't refuse it. I'm a Drewholic. I need help. I want to read other books though. Do you hear what I'm saying?

But, there is one problem though. Ned he is stupid. He does things so stupidly you have to feel sorry for him. He's a real bore and he gives Nancy a bad name. I'd like to kill him off. Do you have a kinda series you read and hate one of the characters?

Sincerely,
Joshua Davidson

2/5/89

Dear Josh,

Hi Josh, nice letter. I love the line about you being a Drewholic. I got a good laugh out of that one. I guess if you have something you just can't live without I guess it would be OK to have that be a favorite series of books.

I'm sorry One Eyed Cat *was so predictable and boring. I guess the topic was OK and would have been better if the author was less predictable in what was going to happen. I know I've asked this before, but have you read* My Teacher the Hawk? *I read it to the class at one time but I don't think you were listening. Maybe you could read it and if you're interested come see me.*

Mr. Nelson

The tone of the letters between child and teacher, teacher and child is quite frank. The letter writing begins in September and continues weekly throughout the year. Some themes and books are the subject of several exchanges. The letters, along with the whole-class sharing and reading by the teacher to the entire class, become a medium of social currency. Because the children read and write about their books—each child averages thirty to forty books over a year's time—book talk becomes a way of life in these classrooms. Reading is thus the means by which children (in this case, every child) has something to contribute to everyone from the books they read.

ACTION: **HELP CHILDREN DISCOVER THAT READING PROVIDES SPECIFIC INFORMATION TO SATISFY A NEED FOR FACTS.**

Mark Milliken, a fifth-grade teacher at Stratham Memorial School, helps children to question their texts. When they do, they find that they need more information, and that requires additional reading. Mark spoke about the change in the children's reading:

MARK: Then we started to see the limitations of the social studies book. It was such a surface approach. It just skimmed the surface of history. Their learning logs dealt with the fact that they wanted to learn more about Incas and Pizarro. So we discussed ways to do that.

When the children did some reading in other reference sources they found that the social studies text ducked the moral issues in what Pizarro did to the Incas. The extent of the exploitation of the Incas was left out of the textbook. Through this experience children learned what reading can and cannot do.

When teachers ask big questions and expand well beyond the confines of the curriculum, extra resources are required. Then children can move into the best uses of reading and find out in a practical, personal way how reading helps them find out what they want to know.

Peter Schiot, a fifth-grade teacher at Oyster River Elementary School in Durham, New Hampshire, moved children into reading and writing in a different way. He teaches fractions and decimals through stock market quotations. Children figure the full value of stocks by noting the daily fractional shifts in quotations. They also shift the fractions to decimals for easier computing. It wasn't long before children began to note which stocks were the gainers and which were the losers.

One day Schiot noted an advertisement in the *Wall Street Journal* announcing the American Telephone and Telegraph Investment Challenge. The challenge offered a fictional $500,000 to college classes to invest in the market. The object was to see how classes can increase the value of a well-selected portfolio in four months. When AT&T allowed Schiot's fifth-grade class to enter, their need for reading resources exploded.

The children began to read *Barron's*, the *Wall Street Journal*, and *Financial Times* in order to study leading market indicators.

They complemented their reading by drawing on human re-sources, using 800 numbers to talk with brokers and inviting local investors and a professor from the university to visit their classroom. Still more reading was needed to understand market shifts and to balance their portfolios more wisely. When the four months ended, the fifth-grade class was 1,500 out of 6,800 entrants.

When children follow up on their need for information, their reading extends well beyond any textbook and their under-standing of what reading is for and what it can do is delightfully enhanced. Drawing up a chart to help children understand the function of reading is a natural and exciting enterprise under these circumstances. Once again, discuss what reading does *after the experience* so that children can consider its value in retrospect, when it can best be understood.

ACTION: HELP CHILDREN UNDERSTAND WHAT READING AND WRITING
CAN DO IN THE WORLD BEYOND SCHOOL.

One way for children to understand the importance of reading and writing in their own lives is to examine how other people use reading and writing. Mary Comstock and Mary Ann Wessells (1989) conducted a study with fifth graders at the Stratham Memorial School to help them probe and begin to understand what reading and writing are for. Comstock and Wessells began with the children themselves, then increased the class's arc of exploration from themselves to others, and then went back to reflect on their own needs as literate learners. The series of ever-expanding questions the children asked themselves were arranged in the following order, with further questions for re-flection:

1. What do you use reading and writing for in school?
2. How are reading and writing used at home?
3. How does your information in question one compare with that in question two?

When the responses were compared the children noted that "while some differences exist between the lists, their nature is more closely tied to setting (for example, reading in order to cook at home or to fill in time logs at school) than to the basic purposes of reading and writing." But, as the researchers noted, "little difference could be seen in their perceptions about what reading and writing were for at home and at school."

They then entered into a new phase of questions that carried them on new journeys of information gathering:

1. How do you think other people, outside of home and school, use reading and writing?
2. When you go on a print search in the room what do you find out about how print is used?

When children answered the first question their lists were quite short. The research team then moved them into question 2, which brought a rich harvest of new insights:

They began with the obvious bookshelves, but soon were peeking under coffee mugs looking for the names of designers, crawling under desks recording inventory numbers and reading the warning inside the heater. . . . although they did not realize it at the time, each of these was evidence of the many literate lives which made our classroom possible.

Children did the same thing at home and expanded their lists still further, realizing in the process that there was a world of print and numbers they still did not understand. Through a series of discussions the children decided that an interview with their parents might elicit the best information. They brainstormed a list of questions to ask the parents who agreed to come into the classroom for an interview. Their questions changed as they became more precise at finding out just how reading and writing were used in their parents' occupations. The researchers noted:

All of the volunteers arrived prepared to be interviewed about reading and writing, as well as to supply additional information about their jobs. Many brought examples of forms, catalogs, pieces of equipment, examples of professional journals, instructional manuals, operating procedure forms and time charge slips.

To complete their study the researchers asked the children to do two layers of reflection on the data:

1. Make a list of what surprised you from the interviews. What uses of reading and writing were new to you?
2. Compare the latest list resulting from the interviews to the original list made from your own classroom perceptions.

When you try this Action you and your class may design a completely different approach to gathering and analyzing the information. Comstock and Wessells constantly pushed the children to come up with their own questions in order to expand their notions of the power of reading and writing.

FINAL REFLECTION This chapter is meant to help us begin to understand the miracle of print. Although we can go through an entire lifetime successfully using print for our own ends, we acquire greater literate power when we understand what happens when we read as well as the many uses of reading that are available to us. We may look to books to make decisions in crisis or to help us deal with grief. We may seek books to gather more information about a problem that confounds us or search out people in new places who are reading books. We know that we need never be alone as long as there are books and people who can share with us their own delight in exploring the world through reading.

shorten conferences

Since 1983, when *Writing: Teachers and Children at Work* was published, the writing conference has borne an enormous amount of weight. In fact, the book gave too much emphasis to the conference. (I'll accept the blame for that; I devoted five chapters to it.) Let me be clear: the conference—the listening stance—is the heart of good teaching. But the place of the conference in the writing process approach needs to be rethought.

We have viewed writing as strictly a one-to-one teaching situation. Although many teachers have shifted from making red marks on papers to handling corrections in conference, the basic philosophy that teaching is synonymous with correcting has remained unchanged. Not many days go by before the teacher says, "How can I get to them all? After two days I've only worked with about six children." Each conference averages about twenty minutes per child.

Again, my own work has contributed to some of the misunderstanding about conferences. Most of the examples in the book showed one teacher with one child. I demonstrated too much of the skills work and the publishing of children's pieces through individual conference structures. Nevertheless, the conference, in which the child speaks and the teacher listens, is still central to my view of effective learning. For this reason, I want to review the elements of the conference to see what should be retained to make it more effective. Once we have determined the essentials, then those aspects of teaching writing that do not belong in the conference can be moved to the classroom contexts where they do belong.

CONFERENCE ESSENTIALS   The writing conference is largely intended to help both you and the child keep in touch with the child's writing. There is a three-dimensional aspect to it: (1) Where did the piece come from? (2) Where is the piece now? (3) Where will the piece be going? Writers write with a sense of the history of the piece

89

and, unconsciously, a sense of their own history as writers. Simple interchanges demonstrate this:

TEACHER: How is it going, Brenda?

BRENDA: Well, pretty good. I'm writing about how we should be allowed to share writing more in other rooms. I need to talk to some other kids to get their opinions.

TEACHER: Who did you have in mind?

BRENDA: Kelly and Jen.

TEACHER: Go to it.

Brenda gives a brief history of her piece, roughly what it is about, and what she is struggling with. Although she does not necessarily know what she will write next, she does have a sense of a solution to her current problem. Brenda knows the classroom structure well enough to decide who can help her, and she also knows that an effective means for gathering data on a classroom issue is to seek out other ideas.

Brenda's method for solving her information problem is born of the hundreds of problems solved every week in the classroom. It is also a major reason for shorter conferences. The child knows she is supposed to be a good problem solver. The teacher is used to delegating. In the illustration above, the issue was not so much giving Brenda permission to consult as it was finding out which classmates Brenda considered effective helpers for her piece.

VOICE AND FLOW   I suspect that about 80 percent of our conferences with children enable them to explain what they are doing. Children can hear themselves talking about the subject and feel their voice controlling the information. If the teacher senses little control, she can ask questions to help the child gain control again. Listen carefully to the child's voice, listening for words, plot, or characters that reveal the child's involvement.

If you sense a teachable moment, which may happen in less than 10 percent of the conferences, do a quick two-minute demonstration. Show the child what you mean in terms of the next step. When the child's plans look good (see Chapter 9), decide what skill is appropriate for the "zone of proximal development" revealed in the conference. Vygotsky (1978) describes this zone as "the distance between the actual developmental level as determined by independent problem solving and the level of potential development as determined through problem solving under adult guidance or in collaboration with more capable peers" (86). That is, we try to sense the teachable moment, the moment when and where learning can best take place. We structure our teaching by showing children steps that will help them learn or perhaps by posing a problem rather than trying to solve one.

Here's an example of how to guide a student to the next step:

TEACHER: How is it going, Nicky?

NICKY: So-so. I can't figure out what to do next, though.

TEACHER: What did you want to do?

NICKY: I think it is time to end it but I can't decide how to do that. I want to have a tricky ending—well, something that leaves them thinking.

TEACHER: What is the piece about?

NICKY: It is about these kids who are lost in the woods and they have survived for four days. They've found a stream that they think will carry them back to civilization. They have seen a helicopter go overhead that was looking for them. But I don't want one of those stupid reunions. In fact, I want the reader to think they'll get out but not be too sure and end it there.

TEACHER: What could you do that would put doubt in the mind of the reader?

NICKY: I know, one of the kids could get sick, real sick on

something he ate and everyone could wonder if he'd get out in time.

Nicky has firm plans, and the teacher merely listens to his concern about how to achieve the kind of effective ending he wants. Nicky actually gives a clue, and the teacher merely bounces the question he is asking himself back to him: "What could you do that would put doubt in the mind of the reader?" Extending a conference when a child has good plans in mind is a good use of conference time. This conference with Nicky is effective because of the other good things happening in the classroom. Children are used to taking responsibility, developing their own plans, and negotiating meaning with others.

In some conferences, teachers deliberately *create problems*.

JENNIFER: I'm done. I'm ready to publish.

TEACHER: How did you decide you were ready?

JENNIFER: I, uh, I finished it.

TEACHER: What did you do to get it ready for publishing?

JENNIFER: Uh, I looked it over, uh . . .

TEACHER: I don't think you are too sure, Jennifer; you check it through carefully. Then who would you like to look it over with you?

JENNIFER: Christy.

TEACHER: Fine. Check it, see Christy, then let me know when you are done, and you can show me how you got ready for publishing.

This conference is short because, as Jennifer knows, there are classroom procedures for preparing for publication. But like many children, she forgot to double-check her conventions prior to publication. Not all children need to consult with others, but in this instance, the teacher thought Jennifer would benefit from knowing she could talk it over with another child. Carefully designed procedures for handling problems by consulting with other children and checking oneself were important for the success of this conference.

Most of the conferences in these examples occurred while the teacher was walking around the classroom. Walking conferences are automatically shorter because the teacher is not sitting, which seems to suggest large amounts of time.

The essentials for a good conference are:

- The presence of speaking, the chance for both child and teacher to hear the child's voice. The teacher listens and follows the child's lead.
- Flow, so that the child's piece continues to move ahead. Questions look for "what will you do next?"
- A more distinctive future. The conference is based on the child's plans.
- Extending the child into new thinking in the zone of proximal development.
- Solutions and then further problems for the learner to consider.

Conferences are shorter and better because of a host of teacher initiatives, many of them based on Actions you have already tried in other chapters. They are of two kinds: surveys of the classroom that affect the length and quality of conferences and the activities that are practiced in the actual conference itself.

ACTION: SURVEY YOUR TEACHING.

Conferences are shorter because you have already assessed the essentials that help to make them effective. Here are some of the areas to assess:

- *Time for writing.* Unless there is time for writing a minimum of four times each week for at least thirty-five or forty minutes, you will feel pressured. If a teacher is in a hurry and not listening effectively, conferences become a waste of time, not unlike the extensive correction of workbooks. Conferences are kept short not because a teacher is in a hurry, but because the teacher focuses on a single issue and lets the child do most of the talking.

- *Child independence.* How much of the classroom structure is organized so that children can function independently? If you are concerned about children's independence, try the Actions suggested in Chapter 3, "Structure a Literate Classroom." The stance of the conference is "this is your piece, you write, you teach, you are in charge." If a sense of independence has not been developed effectively, then children will wait for the teacher to solve problems for them—and conferences will be longer.

- *Examine mini-workshops.* How many skills and tools do you demonstrate in a short workshop format (Chapter 7)? You may feel pressured in conferences because you are trying to teach each child how to spot and eliminate errors in conventions. Small groups or entire room workshops deal with conventions in a more timely way.

- *Review your demonstrations.* When you demonstrate, children have a chance to see and hear the kinds of decisions you make as you compose. They become apprentices to your reflection, revising, questioning, and discovery. The stance is one of "time for thinking"; it is not rushed. This should reduce tension for both the teacher and student and contribute to better listening, which leads to greater ambitions on the part of the children.

ACTION: SURVEY YOUR CHILDREN.

We save time and our conferences become more appropriate when we develop a strategy for selecting which children are in need of them. Not all children's conferences require the same attention. Some sustain their pieces for days, even weeks. Then there are those who seem to stop and start on a daily basis. The "starters" write with little sense of history: each piece begins the moment the child puts his name on the paper. Children who are in this phase of development need to have more conferences. At best, the future for them is uncertain.

Most of the conferences are group conferences in which children with similar needs work together. These kinds of conferences may occur weekly or biweekly as you see the need arising.

Notice that two of the four situation conferences should occur before the children start to write. When children are in the planning stages, your time and the child's are best used, and this will lead to shorter and more efficient conferences later on. If you and the child have made plans together, then your later conferences already have a base of understanding. Furthermore, the earlier you participate in a piece, the more effective your teaching, nudging, and expecting may be later on in the piece.

ACTIONS IN
CONFERENCE

Writing is a craft and teaching it is a craft. Those who work at their disciplines often single out particular tools or skills in their professional repertoire for conscious examination and repetition. When Jane Hansen taught me how to do cross-country skiing, she choose one element in my form, the use of arms and poles, for a twenty-repetition sequence and then shifted off to leg form for another repetition sequence. I concentrate on various elements in my repertoire in order that they may be more effective when I am not thinking of them. If I am to focus completely on the child, and in helpful ways, then I want my own repertoire to be graceful and automatic.

The following Actions contain elements of this kind of "automaticity." They should be essential tools in our teaching repertoire and so well embedded that we have practiced them enough to know their appropriate place in responding to children. These actions are designed for practice, but just enough practice to keep us in touch with the quality of our responsiveness.

ACTION: PRACTICE LISTENING.

Once a month starting now, tape-record a half-hour class period in which you conduct a minimum of five conferences. During these five conferences deliberately focus only on listening. Your task is to try to maximize the child's speaking, to use every means to encourage the child to speak in a ten to one ratio; that is, the child should speak approximately ten times more than you do. Here are some approaches that will help your listening:

• Begin with a child who you sense has plans; the piece is moving. Say, "How is it going?" and wait at least twenty seconds before speaking again.

   Say, "What is your piece about?" and wait twenty seconds.

   Say, "What do you plan to do next?" and wait twenty seconds.
• Restate briefly what a child has said and then move on.
• Above all, help the child to teach you about the topic at hand.

Don't worry about extending ideas or demonstrating, as you would in normal teaching. These sessions are meant to be unusual. You are deliberately learning about your listening and also renewing your understanding of what happens when you listen this intensively. You may feel that such actions on your part will interfere with children's learning, but listening is so rarely done well that both you and the children will thrive on it.

   Good listening is not unlike our first experience in addressing a large audience. In practices, when our coach tells us to speak more loudly, we feel we are shouting because we are so unused to hearing our voice project. The same is true in listening, whether in conferences, marriage, conversations with friends, and so on. When we feel we have listened too much, we are probably just *beginning* to enter the circle of effective listening. Replay the tape and note what seemed to help the child speak; note where you didn't need to speak. Examine the length of your pauses when you wait for the child to speak.

ACTION: EXPLORE THE DIMENSIONS OF A PIECE OF WRITING.

Every piece of writing has a past, a present, and a future dimension. At some point the writer chose a topic or started thinking about a topic. The writer is now engaged in a particular aspect of composing a piece about the topic. The writer also has some sense of future about the piece. I need to have some way of framing the time dimensions of the piece of writing. As I listen to a writer—of any age—I'm trying to construct in my mind the story or history of the piece and the writer's involvement in it.

In this Action, deliberately explore the process dimension of children's writing. Try it several times a month. In a conference, although I try to frame every piece in a narrative history as I listen, I rarely use the actual questions I ask the child about her involvement in a piece all at once.

On the day that you try this Action, let the children know what you are doing. I make the children as much a part of my exploration as possible: "I'm very interested in listening to you tell me about your pieces this morning. I'll be coming to some of you and asking, 'How did you happen to choose this topic and get involved with it? Where are you now, and what will you be doing next with it? You could help me by telling the story of your piece.' "

Here are some of the kinds of questions I ask to explore the history and direction of a piece:

For the past:

- Can you tell me how you happened to choose this topic?
- Can you remember the moment when you first thought of this?
- What did you hope would happen because you wrote this?
- What did you hope to learn?
- Did this have any connection with anything you've written before? Is it anything like a topic you've written about before?
- When did you start this piece?
- Did you run into any stumbling blocks? Anything slow you down so far?

For the present:

- What is the piece about?
- What have you just worked on? What are you working on now?
- How is it going?
- Have you spoken about it with anyone recently?
- How did it go this morning?

For the future:

- What do you think will happen next?
- What will you write next?
- How do you think it will end?
- Who will read this?
- What will you do with it when you finish?
- What will you write next?
- How do you think you will write the next part?

Remember to use only a few questions from each category or children will have every right to be annoyed at the long interruption. I suggest that you learn two or three from each category so that you will not need the list when you confer with the child. Above all, the same principles apply here as in the

Action on practicing your listening: wait at least twenty seconds for the child to speak.

ACTION: PRACTICE DELAY AND REFERRAL.

Sometimes the conference works best when the issue doesn't have to be handled immediately. Turning a problem back to the writer, or to other children in the room, can work better than an immediate demonstration. When children write every day and you regularly make your rounds in the classroom, the pressure to overcorrect or to solve children's problems immediately is reduced. When a child encounters a problem, I start by trying to help the child define it:

TEACHER: How is it going, Ellen?

ELLEN: I'm stuck. I don't know what to do.

TEACHER: What's your piece about?

ELLEN: My brother smokes. It's about him smoking.

TEACHER: How did you happen to write about this?

ELLEN: I know that smoking is bad. It's on the TV all the time. I'm afraid he'll get sick.

TEACHER: Where are you in the piece now? What have you just written?

ELLEN: Well, I just wrote about how smoking is bad.It can give you cancer. And then I got stuck.

TEACHER: What did you hope to say? Did you want to say anything about your brother?

ELLEN: Yeah, I want to tell about him too, but it doesn't fit with this first stuff.

TEACHER: Tell me about your brother and smoking.

ELLEN: He's been smoking for about three months now. I know my mom doesn't know about it and I think she should. I don't know if I should tell her or not. My brother would never speak to me. He'd be mad!

TEACHER: Ellen, it sounds as if you have to settle for yourself about telling. Right now, I'd say forget what you've written so far and write about whether to tell your mother or not. If it makes sense, write about that and then you can see about going ahead.

Notice how the teacher has framed Ellen's problem by finding out about the history of the piece, where she is now, and what she hopes to do with it. In this instance, the teacher diagnoses Ellen's problem as one in which she either doesn't know how to integrate her data about smoking with her brother's situation, or how to deal with the issue of telling her mother or keeping silent about his smoking. It seems that Ellen would benefit from putting her initial attempt aside and writing more directly about how to deal with her parents. Sometimes avoiding writing about large issues can create a block. Ellen may decide she doesn't want to write about her parents and stay with her original approach. Or the teacher may say, "Why not put your piece away for a while?" or, "Is there anyone here in the room with whom you'd like to talk this over?" The process of surveying an issue helps the teacher to make a more effective judgment. Delay or referral in these circumstances is often more effective. It also helps the teacher to "listen through" the process—a specific process.

One other step the teacher might have used in this conference would be data review:

TEACHER: Ellen, your piece is about your brother and smoking. You got into this because of your concern for his health and what you know about cancer. You first wrote some information about cancer and then got stuck, yet you wanted to bring in your brother's problem more. But right now, you just told me about telling or not telling your parents about it. How do you figure you'll handle that?

After this kind of review, it is possible to turn the issue back to the child. Still, the child may not want it back and may require more time to think about it.

Take time to survey the room again to observe how children are consulting with each other. If children have not learned how to consult with each other, they are missing a valuable source of help. Worse, more pressure is placed on the conference the child has with you, the teacher. From September until the last day of school, I work hard to teach children how to help each other. Ask yourself, "How much does the success of writing in this classroom depend on me?" You should be able to think of many contributing factors: the child himself, other children, the opportunity to think a little more about the topic.

ACTION: PRACTICE RAISING YOUR EXPECTATIONS.

It is easy to be lulled by a well-oiled, comfortable learning environment. The folders are full, children chat with each other, writing is published, and skills seem to be making headway. Yet I still find it necessary to make periodic assessments of the level of challenge and self-challenge in the class. As a professional, I also need to maintain an edge of challenge. Several times a month I consciously work on my own ability to challenge children in conferences. If you have not tried the Actions in Chapter 9, you will at least want to read the chapter for background.

An appropriate level of challenge also contributes to a shortening of conference time. You may want to work hardest at helping children to change their own level of self-challenge. As in other Actions that aim to shorten conferences, I prepare by reviewing the children's folders, checking first for children who appear to be ready to raise their own expectations:

- Look for a child who has a strong piece of writing. When a piece is strong, children are more easily challenged.
- Move around the room asking about children's plans—in content, skills, and process. The children know I expect them to make plans, yet some need reminding and more time to reconsider.

Children will share their plans if they know they will get help. They will also share if you take their plans seriously. Sometimes a child's plan may seem less than challenging. If so, look at the level of challenge the child has maintained over an extended period, say, two months.

Children can make realistic, effective plans if their choices are not too numerous, which usually means selecting only one area for help. This is not easy to do, since any piece usually shouts with numerous problems that demand attention. The ability to select and recognize what is important for the child is one of the most challenging areas of growth for a professional. When teachers do not select one skill and instead try to accomplish in the conference what they once did by marking up a child's paper to bring it toward "perfection," conferences automatically get longer. Selection is the essence of the art of writing; selection is also the essence of the art in teaching. As a teacher, my selections get better when the child takes a major role in planning.

ADJUSTMENTS Some children have a problem maintaining a sense of self-challenge. Their ability to make plans is meager. Sometimes this begins at home. Their parenting is autocratic, all challenges come from outside themselves, and all reward systems are external to themselves. I can hear their voices: "Is this any good? What should I do next? Is this spelled right?" Of course, some don't even ask. Instead they cause a disturbance in the classroom. Combine a parenting problem with a history of dependence fostered by specialists and clinics, by extensive correction and little focus on instruction, and even greater problems in developing plans arise.

My approach to helping children learn to develop plans is first to make the child aware of his own effective learning history. The older the child, the longer this takes. Until a child finds out for himself that a particular tool or skill works, he has little sense of his power to learn. Children in this predicament view the teacher's early attempts to point out specific abilities as manipulation: "She just wants to get me to work." These children have not yet found out what writing does (see Chapter 4). When children begin to understand the function of writing and at the same time to develop a sense of their own history as learners, their plans become much more specific and effective.

ACTION: PRACTICE THE TWO-MINUTE CONFERENCE.

The effective two-minute conference represents a coming together of the abilities you have tried in the preceding Actions in this chapter. The two-minute conference seeks to carry out the basic objectives of the conference itself:

- That the child does the most speaking and the teacher listens. Children need to hear their voices, to hear their intentions.
- That the child has a sense of where she has been, where she is now, and where her plans will take her.
- That it be an effective means of demonstrating a new skill, but a skill more closely related to the information, structure, and direction of the piece.
- That it have a dimension of dialogue and expectation.

Bring a readiness to listen extensively, sense where a child is in a piece, demonstrate effective teaching (choosing just one element), and challenge the child in proportion to that child's ability to formulate useful plans. The two-minute conference works when you have effectively surveyed and revised the classroom-based components that contribute to children's independence and self-awareness.

FINAL REFLECTION The Actions in this chapter have pointed toward shorter, more effective conferences. Some conferences are obviously shorter than two minutes: a brief question can show where the child is going, and you move on in a couple of seconds. As the year progresses, conferences become more open and frank as you and the children understand each other better. The higher the level of challenge, the shorter the conference. In addition, the more responsibility children take and the more their independence is respected, the more they will say, "I don't think that will work. I think I'll try it this way," or "Would you please explain that one again? I don't think I understand it." When children know we want to learn from them, we save enormous amounts of time simply because they tell us when they are confused.

One of the more advanced skills in a writer's repertoire is the ability to delete unnecessary information and to enlarge certain other elements in order to expand and clarify meaning. Good conferences are as much a result of what you don't do as what you do: structure the classroom so that children can take responsibility for their learning and thrive on an effective level of challenge.

connect skills with meaning

I bear the scars of skills fanatics. Like many of you, much of my writing has been red-lined to death. In school, no matter how hard I tried for accuracy, there was always someone who had a bigger book of "don'ts" and "should haves" than I did. If I could have walked through the streets shouting, "Unclean, unclean!" I might have felt better. Occasionally I'd get a comment or two about the quality of my ideas, but I can't recall a single instance in which a teacher pointed to the damage my poor conventions did to my information.

In his book *Writing and the Writer*, Frank Smith points out that every act of putting marks on a page is an act of convention. As I sit at my computer putting down these words about skills, every letter that follows every other letter, the spaces in between groups of letters to indicate words, the period or stop to end an idea, the spaces between lines, and the capital letter at the beginning of each sentence are acts of convention. They help you, the reader, enter into a realm of convention that is familiar so you can concentrate on the information without distraction. After all, that's what conventions are for. To help the thoughts in my head reach the page, I choose words and other symbols so that you can compose your own interpretation of what I mean and what you want to understand.

I've used the word *skills* in the title of this chapter with American audiences in mind. In the United States we have a national preoccupation with skills. Like a 1-2-3-4 tract for salvation, *skills* is one of those words that everyone assumes everyone else understands. When I'm asked whether I "believe in skills" during a workshop I immediately respond, "What did you have in mind?"

The response is, "You know, grammar, capitals, possessives." Sometimes the person only means punctuation. I prefer to use the word *conventions* because I think it is more accurate. *Skills* is a much broader term and could include such elements as writing good beginnings and endings, reorganizing texts, or developing characters. These are all important tools to have along with the conventions. A skill is a tool developed artfully over time. The *American Heritage Dictionary* defines it as "1. Proficiency, ability, or dexterity; expertness. 2. An art, trade, or technique, particularly one requiring use of the hands or body." The first meaning of the word hints at the second, a proficiency with something involving the use of the body. According to this definition, we can speak of the skill of handwriting. Within a craft there are skills that require practice; we repeat them again and again until they become almost automatic. The craftsperson works toward a meaningful creation and draws upon many component skills in order to realize the creation in its final form.

Both skills and conventions exist to enhance the meaning the author wishes to express. They are intended as much for the author as for the audience who will read the text. When I write a sentence like "I once knew a man with a wooden leg named Smith" I ought to be as confused about its meaning as the next person. The precise use of pronouns, the marking off of units of meaning with commas, and the provision of specifics for a clearer identification of a character's motives are conventions that will help me to understand my own intentions. I may think I know what I mean, but until I record a sentence with conventional precision in relation to other sentences, I can't be sure I understand what I am trying to say. I may think that I know and feel that I know, but further questioning by friends will reveal that my thinking is muddled.

TAKE THE MEANING ROAD

Yesterday I looked over the transcript of an address I gave at a conference here in New Hampshire. I prepare for an address by going over outline after outline, scrolling images in my mind's eye, even memorizing certain lines I want to deliver with precision. I deliver most of the address, however, without a prepared text. I do this to be able to concentrate on the audience; I feel it helps the audience to understand my ideas better, at least that is my rationalization. The transcript, however, is tough medicine. All the meaning markers I add with my voice (stress, pause, and intonation), hands, eye contact, and posture are lost to me when I read the transcript. People speak of writing as talk written down. My transcript is rude truth that it isn't.

Writers need a thorough knowledge of conventions. They need to put markers in to help the text flow like speech, so that readers feel that the writer is present and talking directly to them as they read. When the writer provides a clear text whose words are well chosen, whose meaning is precise, and whose use of conventions is consistent, the reader can focus on interpreting the meaning of the text.

Conventions help meaning. Try reading the transcript of a conversation between two people without any conventions to guide you:

I think you ought to lose some weight. No, I shouldn't. The trouble with you is you think losing weight is some kind of badge of salvation. Be thin and go to heaven. But you'll be subject to more physical ailments if you don't lose weight. It will be a strain on your heart. But you'll die ten years later than I will and your life will be so boring, all that tasteless, inane stuff going between your teeth will make those extra years as dull as cardboard. But that isn't the choice; dull living and dull food. I have exciting tastes. Prove it.

It is difficult to know who is speaking and when. To solve this problem, writers use new paragraphs every time there is a change in speakers:

I think you ought to lose some weight.
No, I shouldn't. The trouble with you is you think losing weight is some kind of badge of salvation. Be thin and go to heaven.

But you'll be subject to more physical ailments if you don't lose weight. It will be a strain on your heart.

But you'll die ten years later than I will and your life will be so boring, all that tasteless, inane stuff going between your teeth will make those extra years as dull as cardboard.

But that isn't the choice; dull living and dull food. I have exciting tastes.

Prove it.

The meaning is certainly enhanced once you can distinguish one speaker from another. The paragraph, used well, does more to help the meaning of the text for me, the writer, and you, the reader, than quotation marks. Naturally, I'd like to know more about the people speaking; I'll learn more if I identify the speakers with details and use punctuation to separate the details from the actual words they speak. These additions are in boldface:

__Svelte Eve finally addressed her roommate, Sharon.__ "I think you ought to lose some weight."

__Sharon abruptly looked up from her reading.__ "No, I shouldn't. The trouble with you is you think losing weight is some kind of badge of salvation. Be thin and go to heaven."

__The determined lines on Eve's face shifted to concern.__ "But you'll be subject to more physical ailments if you don't lose weight. It will be a strain on your heart."

"You'll die ten years later than I will," __Sharon interrupted__, "and your life will be so boring, all that tasteless, inane stuff going between your teeth will make those extra years as dull as cardboard."

"But that isn't the choice," __Eve sighed__, "dull living and dull food. I have exciting tastes."

"Prove it," __said Sharon, slamming her book closed__.

As I look over the text I notice I have a comma separating roommate and Sharon. The name and the identity are helped by the comma. I have a person and who the person is. The comma clarifies the classification. The quotation marks are especially helpful when I want to separate the actions and the descriptors from the actual words in the conversation. Some might argue, "Well, why do you need quotation marks at the end of one person's speech when you shift to a new paragraph for the next person? You'd know the person had finished speaking." Good point. In fact, the writer William Carlos Williams doesn't use quotation marks in his collection of short stories, *The Farmer's Daughter*. My only response is, "When in doubt, help the reader." Meaning and conventions are connected. Help yourself and the children in your classroom to begin to question how the meaning of a text is enhanced by the use of conventions. Sometimes you may have no clear answers, but you might find it interesting to speculate.

ACTION: USE MINI-LESSONS AND KEEP TRACK OF THEM IN A NOTEBOOK.

Conventions are as much for us as for the children, especially if we try to understand their connection with communication. Pushing our understanding of how they work to enhance a text will clarify our writing. Lucy Calkins, Nancie Atwell, and Mary Ellen Giacobbe have come up with a number of formats to help children to include conventions in their own work. I think the most important one is the mini-lesson in which a specific convention is singled out for attention. This is a well-prepared demonstration of a convention that lasts approximately ten minutes and occurs during most writing sessions. In each case teachers show how the convention clarifies meaning.

Buy a notebook. Make it a supple, three-hole, looseleaf type in which you can keep track of your mini-lessons with the entire class or with small groups. You can insert the material you use for demonstrations or the dated, written plans in your note-book. You can also record the names of the children who at-tended the small group mini-lessons.

Since you put time into planning the mini-lessons you ought to keep a record of them. Sometimes you can use them again; at least keep a detailed enough account to help you when you teach the convention at another time. Think of ways of clas-sifying your mini-lessons for easy retrieval. I frequently make acetates to teach a skill on the overhead projector. (You can purchase three-hole punched plastic sleeves in which you can keep the acetate until you use it again.)

The notebook can also be a useful reference source for chil-dren to use. Although I like children to keep their own records of skills in their writing folders, the notebook can be used as another source for refreshing their memories about lessons they have had in the past.

Mini-lessons are short because they are usually about *one* convention. Children keep lists of conventions that are part of their repertoire; they also make plans about which conventions they wish to learn. I try to survey folders for the conventions children wish to learn and to note when I review their work which ones they need to work on.

ACTION: SET THE TONE FOR CONVENTIONS.

The first mini-lesson can be a demonstration with the entire class using the overhead projector. This session is similar to other demonstrations in which you compose with the children or talk aloud about the decisions you make during the com-posing process. In this Action emphasize the relationship be-tween the meaning of the text and the conventions you use. The tone should be one of discovery, as I tried to demonstrate in the sequence about working with dialogue: *The conventions are there to serve us; they are tools to help us and the readers who will read our text understand what we are trying to say.* If the tone of the mini-lesson is one of preoccupation with accurate use of the convention in a first draft, it will not serve its purpose. The following text should demonstrate what I mean; one part is the written text, the other, my conversation with the class about the use of conventions in the written text.

First, the written text:

Squirrels make me itch. Know why? Have you ever watched them? Take a good look and you'll see their tail, nose, legs, even their fur, all on the jump. That's when they're supposedly sitting still. When they move they scoot, jump, and leap. I have the feeling that something is chasing them, even though I don't see anything. When something is chasing them, that's when I really jump inside. They have a kind of crazy zigzag across the yard, a leap for a tree, and then a zoom up to a lower branch. It is like one of those police car chases I see on TV, cutting this way and that down alleys, around corners, stopping dead and then starting up again.

And my commentary:

DON: Just this morning I looked out my window and watched a red squirrel under my bird feeder. Have you ever watched one? Try it. You'll see all parts of the squirrel moving at one time. To get the meaning I want, I'll show all the parts that are moving at one time. See, that will get the itch effect I want. [*I might ask the class what they've seen moving when a squirrel sits. If they have a list I'll use it.*]

Then there's this sentence:

Take a good look and you'll see their tail, nose, legs, even their fur, all on the jump.

I wanted a list all in one sentence because that's the picture I want, a lot of things happening at one time. But I'm going to put these commas in there to make that sentence twitch a little; the commas will separate all those twitching things so we can keep them straight. Now let's read it with the commas in and see if you can feel that squirrel doing all those things at one time.

I've also tried to capture the squirrel's rapid motion through another kind of phrase listing separated by commas: Notice:

- zigzag across the yard
- leap for a tree
- zoom up to a lower branch

or showing they are like police cars:

- cutting this way and that down alleys
- around corners
- stopping dead
- then starting up again

Can anyone think of an animal or something that has a lot of things happening at one time? Make a list and experiment with a sentence. (The serial comma could just as well be used in a list of things I possess or a series of places I've visited.)

The children may wish to take a piece of scrap paper and experiment while we are working. In fact, I find it useful for children to have scrap paper handy so they can doodle or practice conventional tools during the mini-lesson. The serial comma example about the squirrel didn't occur to me until I had written it. I simply asked, "What's going on here? How is this punctuation helping what I'd like to happen?" Start talking aloud or questioning your own punctuation and you'll discover a vast array of tools out there that can clarify what you are trying to say.

EXAMPLES OF OTHER
CONVENTIONS

The actual number of conventions and tools that might be useful in a mini-lesson is infinite. The ones that follow demonstrate a repertoire of tools that enhance meaning.

The colon

The colon, like the comma, the period, and the semicolon, is a punctuation mark intended to stop the reader or to separate ideas into component parts. A few years ago I noticed that a young first grader had used a colon in her writing. She wrote, "There are many kinds of whales: humpback whales, blue whales, and sperm whales." I had never seen a first grader use a colon and wondered what she understood about its meaning. I pointed to the colon and asked, "What's that? What do you call it?"

"You know!" she responded indignantly. Her look said, another foolish question by a researcher. Sensing that she might not know the name, yet noting the accuracy of its placement, I then asked, "What's it for?"

"Oh, that means more to come," she mumbled diffidently, an answer that could have come from any textbook on punctuation. The colon, like the comma in a series, allows us to list information in a short space. Both the writer and the reader can benefit when a lot of information is available in a compact form.

Let me mention a quick example. When I go skiing I often forget things. If I get to where I'm going to ski and find that I have left something behind, I get very angry with myself. I should always check to be sure I have these items: gloves, ski poles, skis, small pack, extra wax, hat, boots, and extra shirt. If I group all those items together after the colon, maybe it will help me remember everything next time.

The period

The period is one of the most difficult forms of punctuation for children to add to their repertoire of conventions. They often have trouble understanding when one idea ends and the next one begins. Yet any number of textbooks and curriculum guides, in an attempt to be systematic, state that the period is the form of punctuation you should teach first. First graders, who usually compose one sentence to go with a picture they have drawn, seem to pick up the notion of a sentence naturally. But the minute they join two ideas or sentences end to end on the same page, periods go out the window. It is not unusual to find high school and college students who are still puzzling over how to mark off their ideas.

The sentence is a meaning unit containing the doer (subject) and the action (verb): "He crossed the room. He ran. She sews." These are the simple ones. When we have a more complex idea to express, things become more difficult: "I'd like to go downtown to pick up a book so that when the snow comes tonight I won't be stuck tomorrow for something to do." I could write, "I'd like to go downtown," and put the period after "downtown." That would be a sentence. What's left ("to pick up a book so that when the snow comes tonight I won't be stuck tomorrow for something to do") isn't a sentence, and that can be the hard part for children to understand.

That's where demonstrations come in, to show what goes together and how. As we look at the remaining half of the sentence above, I'll probably ask the class, "Anything missing here? Anything you want to know?" Some children, because they already know the first part of the sentence, find it difficult to understand that adding a period to the second part does not make it a sentence. It needs a verb to be a sentence. Again, of all the forms of punctuation, the period places the highest demands on both writer and reader. Young writers—and their teachers—need more patience in learning how to use the period as a sentence marker than they do in acquiring just about any other tool in the writer's repertoire.

The comma   The wonderful part about commas and the other forms of punctuation that slow down ideas is the way they mark off the pictures in the mind, like frames in a film. Commas keep one meaning unit from interfering with the next. They help us to clarify imagery and maintain the logic of our thoughts in a good argument. They provide separate rooms in the house of meaning. Their position, laid end to end on a line, keeps things in just the right order so readers will not be too confused by a change in decor from one room to the next. Yet there are times (a moment of anguish or surprise, for example) when I want a grating change of scene—from the quiet of the drawing room to the bustle of the kitchen—and the comma, put in just the right place, helps me to signal readers that I am shifting their attention.

Commas keep things straight. They keep subordinate ideas in their places so that we can understand the main ideas they support. Ideas sometimes have "interruptors" that serve as asides to the reader. Here's an example:

When Howard Baker, the former Republican majority leader in the Senate, was made chief of staff, I heaved a sigh of relief.

In this instance, I felt the need to explain who Senator Baker is.

There are many more reasons for using commas than I have mentioned here. I have simply tried to show how they function to order information so the reader can follow our line of thought.

ACTION: HELP CHILDREN SPECULATE ABOUT CONVENTIONS.

Learning is embedded in the ability to hypothesize. Children need to practice predicting where conventions need to be placed in a text. In your mini-lesson on the overhead projector or the chalkboard, ask children to speculate with you about where certain conventions are needed. (The acetate you prepare for the overhead can become a permanent record of the lesson. It can also be copied and immediately mounted on the bulletin board as a reference for you and the children.) Ask them why they think the meaning of the text will be enhanced by their judgments.

In my demonstration I compose but leave out the conventions, and stop after I've written enough text to ask for their comments:

I get burned up when my team the red sox doesn't sign their best players this spring my favorite roger clemens hasn't been signed and everyone knows how valuable he is to the team and i wonder if the red sox will ever wake up and

Commentary:

DON: Yes?
CHILD: I think you should put something after players.
DON: Why would you put something there?
CHILD: I don't know. It just seems right, that's all.
DON: Sometimes wanting to put something in a place is just a hunch and that's where good experiments start. Anyone like to help out?
CHILD: I think it should go there because you started talking about something new. They didn't sign Roger Clemens.
DON: Okay. So I started something new. How is the period going to help you, the reader?

Hypotheses begin as hunches—here, the gut feeling that something belongs without knowing why or whether it should be a period, a comma, or a question mark. But it begins with the idea that *something* ought to go there. Next comes the notion of how the convention helps the writer or reader, which helps children determine the appropriate mark.

This approach is designed to help children start thinking

about *listening to their texts* so that they can assess which conventions they need and where. By being generally aware as they work through a draft, children learn how to be more precise during their final edit.

ACTION: SHARE CONVENTIONS.

This action is a mini-lesson in which children share information about the different conventions they are using in their writing. As in other sharing sessions, we gather around, look over our writing, and talk about different conventions. This discussion can also be a five-minute segment of a regular sharing time. As the teacher, I also share my own writing. There are several ways I can do this:

1. Mention a convention, read a section of my writing in which the convention is used, and tell how the convention acts as an aid to meaning.
2. Mention a convention I have used but not why I used it. Ask the children for their thoughts about it.
3. Find the same convention as #1 in a trade book and state how the convention clarified the writer's meaning.
4. Point out marks and other conventions the children do not understand. "What's that? I've never seen it before. What's it for?"

Keep records of who participates. Put a list of conventions and who knows how to use each one on the bulletin board (or keep it in a bound folder). In this way children know which of their classmates to consult if they wish to find out about a particular convention. They should also have access to photocopies of past mini-lessons. These can be kept in a folder with a table of contents in the front so children can locate specific conventions more easily.

ACTION: ASK DIFFERENT CHILDREN TO INTERVIEW.

Children should be more aware of which conventions are being used in the classroom—and by whom. Each week, one or two children could move around the room with their folders interviewing other children to see if they have experimented with any new conventions.

ACTION: USE TRADE BOOKS TO DEMONSTRATE CONVENTIONS.

Trade books are an excellent resource for finding and discussing conventions. In this mini-lesson, I want children to notice how professional writers use conventions to enhance the meaning of their texts. I take a paragraph and make a copy of it on an acetate for the overhead projector. Then I ask the children to examine the paragraph for these elements:

- Kinds of punctuation marks.
- Use of nouns and verbs, pronouns in relation to nouns, adverbs in relation to verbs.
- How each convention clarifies the writer's meaning.
- What might be misunderstood if the convention were not present.
- How a convention may have been deliberately broken and how this did or didn't help (as in a sentence fragment).
- The use of language, particularly strong verbs.

This particular mini-lesson with trade books could also be used as backup for other lessons about conventions.

ACTION: WORK ON SCHEDULING MINI-LESSONS.

First, consult with the children. If they know you expect them to have plans for their writing (see Chapter 9), they will be more aware of which conventions they need to learn and which approaches to writing will help them. Refer back to the second

Action in this chapter ("Set the Tone for Conventions"), since children will be continually exposed to new tools they can use in their writing.

Mini-lessons are closely connected with Actions, the heart of this book. Although the Actions in this chapter have been largely connected with conventions relating to punctuation, they can apply to just about any tool a writer uses. Here is a partial list:

- leads
- organization
- editing
- character development
- revising
- endings
- choosing a topic
- dialogue
- proofing
- issues of plausibility
- use of verbs
- use of adverbs
- use of nouns
- use of adjectives
- sentence combining
- planning fiction
- use of capitals
- letter writing
- possessives
- storytelling
- poetry
- argument

After consulting with the children on Friday, I take their folders home over the weekend and look through them for examples of conventions that are teachable and within what

Vygotsky calls the child's "zone of proximal development." Some of the children will have needs that are broadly based, and a demonstration for the entire class will be fruitful. Others will benefit from mini-lessons with clusters of five to eight children.

As I schedule the mini-lessons for the week, I combine children's requests with my observations from the folders. On Monday, I post the schedule on the board. It lists the type of mini-lesson and the day of the demonstration. The mini-lesson in the small-group format is both voluntary and required. In this way, although some children are expected to attend, those who may have a current need for the convention can select it.

In the course of a month, I usually schedule a minimum of sixteen or twenty mini-lessons. Because a running record of each mini-lesson is posted on the board and a copy of the acetate is available in a folder, children can refer back to a particular mini-lesson when they need to. Some mini-lessons may be repeated in a month's time; others will recur about every three months.

In my mini-lesson notebook I keep a record of which children have attended the smaller sessions and which have demonstrated an ability to handle the convention under discussion. At the same time, I recognize that, although proficiency in a tool can be demonstrated, mastery of the tool is another story. When the topic is difficult and the need for information extensive, conventions suffer. And when an idea is not clear to the writer, the writer's language will often become confused, full of convoluted sentence structure and poor punctuation.

In a well-structured classroom, where children are expected to take responsibility for their learning and writing tools are constantly demonstrated, children will be able to help each other. I frequently refer children with problems to others in the room for help. Most of the time they already know who can help them.

ACTION: HELP CHILDREN CONDUCT MINI-LESSONS.

Children should be able to assist in mini-lesson demonstrations. Select a child to work with you as you prepare the lesson. Then, as you go through the steps involved in teaching a mini-lesson, the child will become more proficient in offering advice to classmates through the informal classroom network. The basic steps I point out include the following:

1. Select one tool for demonstration.
2. Define what the tool is for and how it enhances the meaning of the text.
3. Show what you mean by composing an example or by selecting a sample passage from an earlier piece.
4. Involve the other children in the demonstration; let them apply the tool.

The child I select to teach the mini-lesson may have already demonstrated a knowledge of the tool or may be ready to learn it. Teaching the tool may lead to acquiring it.

FINAL REFLECTION Conventions belong to all of us. In acquiring them we gain the power to say new things, extend our meaning, and discover new relationships between ideas. For too long teachers and editors have stood guard over conventions, as if they were esoteric knowledge available only to the few. Seldom did children see their teachers demonstrate how they used conventions where they belong—in writing—or ponder how to use a convention to say something more clearly or more effectively. Conventions are tools we, as teachers, want to give away. The more we give them away through mini-lesson demonstrations, the more children will regard them as a vital part of their writer's repertoire.

look for potential

"Everyone has potential." Trite words. And they can be a curse. A friend of mine was told at a young age that he had an IQ of 130. His teachers kept telling his mother, "Mark has great potential, but he isn't working up to capacity." Easy to say. Who *is* working up to their potential? I'm not, and it bothers me. In my mind I see poems I haven't written and photographs that could win me a Pulitzer Prize (if only I had my camera with me). I know I could write a novel, but I don't. A doctor friend told Don Murray, a Pulitzer-Prize-winning journalist, that when he retired he was going to write a novel. Murray told the doctor that when *he* retired he was going to become a surgeon. We all make statements like the doctor's knowing full well we can talk a good game. In fact, realizing our potential often seems an impossible fantasy. In this chapter we will start to do something about it.

We don't believe people who point out our abilities—most of the time. I used to think it was laziness, but not any more. Now I think that we've been brainwashed by our schooling to be nonbelievers in ourselves. Hence the fantasy of talking about what we *could* do.

Back in 1959 I took a master's course in educational research with Professor Jordan Fiore at Bridgewater State College. He was a well-published historian, and I did careful research in writing a paper I titled "Leo Tolstoy, Neglected Educator." I got a note back: "Publish this piece." Up to that point I had thought well of Dr. Fiore. I was flattered, but I thought his praise misguided and uninformed. Seven years before, as an undergraduate, I had been put on academic probation. In fact, through most of my school years, my papers had been scarred by "help." Five years after I wrote my paper Norman Wiener published his book, *Leo Tolstoy—On Education*. Not until fifteen years after Fiore spoke to me, at the age of forty-three, would I have the courage to submit an article for publication and then, only because Janet Emig encouraged me.

125

I try to do with my graduate students what Janet did for me. About 10 percent of them publish their pieces; another 20 to 30 percent do not believe me when I tell them their writing should be published. I'm sure there are many reasons for not carrying pieces further, but I have a strong hunch that most do not because of their own writing history. There is also a sense of professional inferiority that seems to go with teaching. "Publish? Me? Are you kidding? I'm just a teacher." Fortunately, more teachers are publishing. Their sense of authority is rising and their potential is being realized more than ever, and not just in writing. But the exciting part about writing is that it shows potential in action, where it belongs.

ACTION: FIRST EXAMINE YOUR OWN POTENTIAL.

Before you become involved in the first Action, I'd like you to rethink the meaning of that easy word, *potential*.

We forget the physical side. I remember watching a severely spastic quadraplegic woman trying to scratch out a word, working against the reflex action that turned her head away. She was persistent and got the word down. I've even seen someone write by moving his head with the pencil between his teeth. In *The Man Who Mistook His Wife for a Hat*, Oliver Sacks tells the stories of individuals who have lost the human abilities I've always taken for granted: the power to recognize another human face, a sense of personal history, or the ability to know where one's body is in space.

I reach down and pick up a pen with my right hand. With my left hand I pick up a piece of paper. The room is warm, just comfortable; the light is bright, and the white paper sits on the desk waiting for my thoughts. Sixteen years of schooling gives most of us the words, the spelling, the method of ordering our ideas to affect someone else with our thinking. Yet it astonishes me that print appears on the page when my mind commands my fingers to write. All of these are miracles: paralysis-free fingers; the affluent comfort of light, paper, pen; the ability to see the paper, or a way of getting glasses if I can't; my body upright with no support from braces. This morning a pelican flew by my seventh-story hotel window at St. Petersburg Beach, and I can write about it here on my computer. You, meanwhile, wherever you are in this world, and at a time of your choosing, can create the image that lets you see my pelican. Miracles all. That potential is in all who read these words.

Read Lewis Thomas's (1984) or Richard Selzer's (1979) accounts of human potential from a physician's point of view and the miracle of human capabilities unfolds still further. Human potential begins to take on a much larger scope. The contributions we can make to ourselves and to others are limitless. Life is too short not to consider them.

ACTION: FIND THE WRITER'S POTENTIAL.

One of the easiest and most important ways to discover a writer's potential is to get a glimpse into the thinking of that writer. Just a few days ago, the importance of a child's insight into his own composing was brought home to me by Dan Ling Fu of the People's Republic of China, now a doctoral student at the University of New Hampshire. Last June she was joined by her seven-year-old son, Xiao Di, who entered second grade in the fall with no knowledge of English. Since his arrival he has maintained a writing folder.

In order to get a sense of what Xiao Di valued in his work, Dan Ling asked him to "choose the pieces from your folder that show best how you learn." She wasn't sure that he could do it, since he had spent most of his life in China, where a sense of self tends to be discouraged. At first he thought the directions called for selecting one piece. "I can't do it," he responded. "There isn't one piece that represents me." When he found that he could choose as many as he wished, he care-

FIGURE 8–1   ONE OF XIAO DI'S EARLY WRITINGS (SEPTEMBER)

Xiao-Di (Hanye)		Xiao-Di (Imrk)
我喜欢画画。		1. I like pekhr.
我喜欢朋友。		2. I like fruand.
我喜欢妈妈。		3. I like man.
我喜欢猫。		4. I like cat.
我喜欢爸爸。		5. I like fadr.
我喜欢猴子。		6. I like mang ke.
我喜欢老师。		7. I lke tehr.
我喜欢狗。		8. I like Dog.
我喜欢沙鱼。		9. I like shrk.

fully chose thirteen pieces from the folder. The selections ranged in date from his second week of school in September to the last day of March.

Commenting on three of his choices from September and October (one of which is shown in Figure 8–1), he had this to say:

XIAO DI: They are my early writings. The first time I learned to sound out words. Though they were all wrong, they were still good. That was my first try. And I wrote the Chinese words and drew pictures there too. If people couldn't understand my spellings, they could read Chinese and look at the pictures.

Xiao Di recognizes that errors naturally accompany learning, that they are strong indicators of learning potential. He made another choice, however, that surprised us all and revealed the kind of personal potential that might elude us if we didn't give children an opportunity to choose their best work. Xiao Di chose a drawing of his teddy bear as an important selection for his portfolio (Figure 8–2). Here's why he says he chose it:

XIAO DI: This is a picture I drew out of my head. I didn't copy anything. I mean I drew it without looking at anything. It is just like my own teddy bear. Look at the lips; I like them. I also like the tie; that makes him look great. The other pictures I did out of my head were not as good as this one. This one is really like a real one, as it looks at me with feelings. I just like to draw animals.

Without Xiao Di's explanation of the reasons for his selection, his sensitivity to feelings and their representation in art would be lost to us.

Xiao Di's choice of the best piece among the thirteen was a story he had written at home on the computer.

FIGURE 8–2   XIAO DI'S TEDDY BEAR

THE DOG AND HIS FREND

Once upon a time there was a dog. He wanted a friend, but his mum didn't want her own son to go by himself. But the dog cried all day, so his mum let him go.

So there he was in the woods. And he saw a wolf. He got so happy because he saw that was a friend. So they both got to the wolf's house. The wolf said: "you can stay here." So the dog stayed there for a year. But he missed his mum.

So he went home, and he saw his mum crying. Because he was not home for a year. Then he forgot to go back to wolf's house. The wolf was so angry, and the wolf wrote a letter to the dog. The letter said: "you have to come before the weekend is coming. If you don't, then we are going to have a fight."

And the dog saw the letter, but he forget to go back. So they are going to have a fight. The fight was start, dog's mum was there too. the wolf bite dog's tail, dog bite wolf's nick. And the wolf die. and the dog still finding the frend. And his mum got home.

Now the dog find a grold [girl] dog. Then they got married. they had a boy puppy. They was haply ever after. buthe miss the wolf too. Because the wolf is his frend too.

THE END

Xiao Di's criteria for selecting the piece reveal still further his sensitivity to characterization, to fiction as a genre, and to the basic ingredients contained in fiction. Why did he choose the piece?

XIAO DI: It is long, the longest story I ever wrote, and longer than some other kids' stories in the class. I like the title and words I used in the story. I also liked the ending; it's a happy ending and funny too. This is the first story I did on the computer; I was proud of myself. I really like it.

Since Xiao Di had had two books published in hardcover in class his mother asked, "And you like this better even than these two published books?"

XIAO DI: Yeah, because it is longer than them; the words are better. It has three characters. If you have more characters your story can be long. And the title is better than those stories too.

Although for Xiao Di length is an essential characteristic of good writing, he introduces enough other elements into his discussion (title, characters, humor, ending) to show his potential as a writer. His understanding of story ingredients is something on which a teacher can build. Even more, his sensitivity to feelings in himself and in the characters he writes about is one of the best predictors of long-term writing success. Most fiction written by young children, especially by boys, places action above character. In fact, when characters do appear, they rarely express feelings.

ACTION: LOOK FOR POTENTIAL IN A FOLDER.

Potential can sometimes be seen better in retrospect. Take a broader, longer-term look at how children change. It is better if you wait a minimum of three months before looking at the folder collection. Brenda Miller Power brought an analysis of one first-grade child's folder to me one day and opened my eyes to the possibilities of folder analysis. What follows is some of what we learned about Kelsey Taylor.

I look first for the child's use of specifics—in artwork and in text—but over time. I look at the ups and downs but always from the vantage point of what the child is trying to do. Notice the differences in the following two pieces. In the first, Kelsey had just read a book about the human body provided by her mother:

This is a body [cross-section of skin, well-drawn]. *What you are like in a body. I have been interested in bodies. My mom got us a book about bodies. Bodies are nice. I love to read the books that have bodies in them.*

Although Kelsey is very much interested in science, this is an attempt to write about a book from the outside. She is struck by the importance of the book to her. It may be that she just wishes to share the fact she has read a book about bodies with her friends. In short, the piece is a springboard for further conversation.

Kelsey's next science piece was written as part of a field trip to the beach. Each child could choose something she saw, read about it, and then write about it. Notice the difference in her use of specifics and in her voice as a writer:

Seagulls like to eat scraps of dead fish and shrimp and clams and of course popcorn. They like the tide to bring food. They are white and black. The baby's are dull brown.

Here is a personal piece she wrote about her new bicycle. It is filled with specifics, easily recalled because they happened to her:

I like my bike. I went riding on the highway. I rode around the loop. I was on Garrison. My bike is purple and blue and white. I hate my banana seat. My grandparents gave me my bike for Christmas but I got it on Saturday the eighth of March. Everybody has a bike in my family. On Easter we went riding and we had a snack. On the way back I rode over a snake. It was a garter snake. Me and my sister Alexia know how to pick up snakes. Alexia and Mommy have a 10 speed. I have no speeds.

The details include colors, time markers (Saturday the eighth of March), the banana seat (and her feelings about the seat), the name of the street on which she was riding, the name of the snake, her sister's name, and so on. Consider, however, the next piece that Kelsey wrote, a first attempt at fiction about something she knows: bicycles.

AN OLD BIKE MEETS A NEW BIKE

There was an old bike. It was a very old bike. One day the old bike met a new bike. The new bike said, "Hi" to the old bike. The old bike said "hello" to the new bike. The new bike said, "Let's be friends." So they became friends and lived happily ever after.

In her story, Kelsey demonstrates an understanding of story-telling ingredients: character identification, an exchange between characters, a problem resolved, and a happy ending. The title suggests the essential action, "An Old Bike *Meets* a New Bike," and that not much more is going to happen. This is a piece written from the outside. That is, she sees two bicycles "over there." Yet she demonstrates here her basic knowledge of the fiction genre. How easy it would be for someone to say, "She isn't ready for fiction yet; the specifics are very poor." On the other hand, there are important specifics of another type. Form dominates content, as indeed it must when a writer is just starting out.

On March 10 Kelsey wrote a piece that is a combination of "outside-inside." Kelsey noticed some pictures of herself as an infant in contexts she could not remember. She asked her mother about them and proceeded to use what her mother told her in her own piece. The first part is filled with the same time markers as the bicycle piece:

I was born on May 3 in 1979 one Thursday at 6:55 p.m. I stayed at Exeter hospital in New Hampshire for fourteen hours.

Alexia was born on November 26, 1976 in Corvalis, Oregon on a Friday at 7:29 p.m.. My sister's ears stuck out when she was a baby.

Mom was born in D.C. on April 2, 1948. Daddy was born in Oakridge, Tennessee.

When I was born my right foot turned in. I had to wear a cast for six months. My cast went to my toe and to my knee. When I got my cast I was six months old. When they took my cast off I was seven and a half-months old. When they took my cast off I didn't want it off.

Through her mother's help, Kelsey transformed outside data into personal narrative and thus incorporated it into her current consciousness.

Like most six-year-olds, Kelsey reveals the usual struggle between what is real and unreal, between darkness and light, between self and others. Kelsey chose to write about this struggle with a mixture of specific details and general reactions. The struggle shows in this piece:

An imaginary picture makes me happy. This imaginary picture is pretty. An imaginary picture is not real. When you have a birthday it is real. My birthday is on May 3. It is real. It is an imaginary picture. It makes me happy too.

Kelsey is sharing the fact that both the real and the imaginary can be pleasing, but just how she finds hard to express through words alone.

Kelsey also tries out a bit of literary criticism. After she saw the movie *Peter Pan*, she wrote a piece that combined personal narrative and a suggestion of criticism:

I went to Peter Pan. I like the part when John did the flips in the air. Peter Pan was a girl. Wendy was a girl.

ACTION:　EXAMINE CHILDREN'S USES OF WRITING.

Children show us their greatest potential in their growing understanding of what writing is for. (See Chapter 4 for a more detailed investigation of this subject.) Through her writing folder Kelsey shows us that writing is distinctly connected with her life, interests, reality, and imagination. Most of all, she experiments with new forms, an essential part of anyone's learning profile. She has tried:

- Science writing.
- Personal narrative.

- Personal narrative with interview.
- Fiction—early form.
- Review—early form.
- Philosophy—early exploration of what is real, unreal.

She has also used writing in ways not described in this chapter: notes to friends, collaborative writing with a friend, a nonfiction piece about the school that involved interviewing. With the exception of the gull piece, which she completed after the field trip to the shore, all of Kelsey's writing and exploration were self-assigned.

The potential revealed in Kelsey's pieces did not occur in a vacuum. She is a student in Pat McLure's first-grade classroom at Mast Way School in Lee, New Hampshire, a classroom where literate activity is highly valued and where writing is actually *needed* in order to function in science, in reading, and in response to personal and group events.

Take four writing folders home tonight and examine each child's pieces for their collective breadth and depth in their use of writing. What situations in class led to different types of writing? Children should have experienced situations that prompted them to write letters, observe phenomena, express opinions about events, try out poetic forms, and write some fiction.

I look to see if the forms I have demonstrated in class are reflected in the children's selections. Although most of the writing is unassigned, I do expect children to try different forms. I am constantly trying to nudge children into new topics and new uses of writing.

THE RETROSPECTIVE CURRICULUM

Not all of the writing in Pat's room is as detailed or as broad in its use of different forms of writing as Kelsey's. The process of reviewing a folder like Kelsey's, along with a good cross-section of the writing of other children, will reveal a far more detailed use of curriculum than we could ever design in advance. Because of the work of Brenda Power in this regard, I began to grasp the notion of "retrospective curriculum." In a sense, this is the *real* curriculum, the "what happened?" curriculum, the one we need to evaluate more thoroughly than the prescriptive curriculum concocted in the absence of real data about what children can actually do. And as long as the curriculum is prescriptive, we will continue to underestimate what children can do.

ACTION: LOOK FOR A CHILD'S POTENTIAL IN VERY SHORT OR ABANDONED PIECES OF WRITING.

Our ability to sense potential is frequently challenged by the very short selections written by children who see little worth in their writing. I remember one sixth-grade boy who struggled with writing, hated it, and showed his feelings in an abbreviated scrawl. Five to ten minutes into writing time he'd be staring listlessly out the window or drumming his desk top with a pencil.

One day he wrote, "My fish was biger than peteys." Then, as usual, he stopped. I thought to myself, "I've got to look for potential. His face certainly shows he doesn't think he has any." My first move is to look for specifics. I look for the nouns (fish, peteys—I guess that "petey" is a noun). Then I try to get the nouns in motion by looking at the verbs. In this instance, "was" doesn't provide much motion. Here is my recollection of our conference:

DON: I see you have a fish.
ANDY: Yeah.
DON: How did you get it?
ANDY: Well, I caught it.
DON: Oh, I didn't know you fished. So how did you catch him?

ANDY: Down at Prout's Brook. I caught him in the bend where the deep water is.

DON: So you caught him in the deep part. I was wondering what kind of fish he was.

ANDY: A trout, a brown trout. That's the only kind worth catchin' there.

DON: So how do you catch a brown trout where the deep water is?

ANDY: Well, there's a cut in the bend and you have to go up the brook and let your line drift down into that cut. Browns are smart; you can't let your shadow go over the surface, so you go up the brook. That's where I caught him.

DON: You know just what to do: drop your line up the brook, have it drift down into the deep part and not make a shadow.

In this instance I helped Andy to teach me about trout fishing. I took his few surface clues and probed for a sense of process, some sequence that would help the nouns to move into a narrative. Finally, for both Andy and me, I confirmed the details and the process of his knowledge about catching brown trout.

Everyone has a story to tell. For many the story is trapped inside a single line waiting for someone to release its potential. Andy chose to write, "My fish was biger than peteys." He wanted to write about fishing but started with the final line, either because he didn't know how to begin or because he was reluctant to reveal his writing problems by starting at the beginning of a longer piece.

Christopher, a first grader, finally wanted to share with his class. When he came to sharing time, he had a mass of squiggles with three words underneath: "the bg fel." The other children in Pat McLure's class were skilled enough in receiving pieces and in asking questions to keep Christopher talking about the information contained in the words "the bg fel." They helped Christopher to go on to tell about where the field was, how he and his family hiked in it, and how he played games there with his friends. Although Chris didn't write all that he said, or even a partial account, his knowledge and his potential skill in narrative were revealed to him and to the class. The more extended writing came later.

POTENTIAL: SEVENTH-GRADE CHILD

Sean is a young adolescent with learning problems; he has struggled with writing, but he is in a classroom where students' voices grow so strong they affect everyone. The teacher, Linda Rief, writes with her students and helps them to help each other. Sean wrote this piece:

MY DAD IN THE VIETNAM WAR

This story is really hard for me to write. Its about my Dad who was in the Vietnam War. All the terrible things that happened. How he lost really good friends. Or about one day when my Dad was in a Bar. And some kid rolled alive grenade in. It lucky did not exsplode. Or how he would be walking down the street and a Religious monk who had drenched himself with gasoline, would light a match and burn himself to death just because he was protesting. This year at my Dads birthday, my sister and her friend bought my Dad a book on the Vietnam war. My Dad was happy and sad at the same time. My Dad didn't want to talk about it because he had to maney bad feelings. Someday when my Dad can talk about it. I hope he talks to me.

It would be easy to overlook Sean's potential and be distracted by the sentence fragments, misspellings, and lack of paragraphing. But the power of the story and Sean's selection of essential details in telling about his father's pain and what happened to cause that pain speak of a writer with a strong voice.

ACTION: POINT OUT THE SPECIFICS OF POTENTIAL.

Good teachers are good historians. Teachers accurately observe the unfolding of children's learning histories and then help them acquire a sense of their own learning history by revealing it to them. Kelsey shows what she knows about seagulls, cycling, and her early years. Pat McLure confirms her knowledge and her feelings, and asks questions to help Kelsey see how she understands her material. As Pat does this, she contributes to Kelsey's conscious knowledge of her learning history so ably begun by her parents.

As the child discovers her potential for learning, the teacher discovers her own potential as a teacher and develops her own sense of history as a professional. And the history is specific. The detailed nature of Kelsey's thinking—in speech and in writing—and the changes that occur in those language areas also reveal the professional's own growth. When children cannot reveal their potential, your own potential as a teacher also remains hidden.

When Linda Rief read Sean's piece, she sensed his understanding of Vietnam and of his father's anguish, as well as his own sense of accomplishment in sharing his insights with classmates. In doing so, Linda confirmed the value of her painstaking help as she moved into a new territory of listening and understanding; her own potential as a professional was further revealed to her. In one sense the "proximal zone" of both child and teacher overlapped and, for both, learning occurred. And that is the celebratory side of teaching and learning.

In *Writing: Teachers and Children at Work* (pp. 22–28), I asked teachers to list children's names in one column, to note what each child knows (unique to that child) in a center column, and to make a checkmark in a third column if the child knew that the teacher knew about the special knowledge. In short, the child has confirmation of his knowledge. That exercise is just a beginning. As children speak in conferences and teachers say things like

- What do you do on your own now that you used to need help with?
- Tell me about what other children help you with now and what they used to help you with.
- Tell me what you help other children with now.

even more important knowing and learning are revealed to both.

ACTION: ASK ABOUT THE FUTURE.

As children develop a learning history and gain a stronger sense of what they know and how they know it, their plans for future learning become more detailed. They know the topics they want to write about, the books they want to read, and the specific skills they'll need to accomplish their objectives. The most secure learners will have plans. Ask them:

- What are you going to write about next?
- What is going to happen next in this piece?
- What are you going to read next?
- What can I help you with next? What do you think you'll need to know or be able to do in order to accomplish your next objective?

When children are able to articulate specific plans, they demonstrate to themselves and to you the direction of your mutual potential. But if they have no long-term, present-tense confirmation of their learning and have not experienced a positive learning history, your questions about their future plans may inspire puzzlement and discouragement in both of you.

GETTING THE BUGS OUT As children grow older, confirmation of potential can be frightening. In view of their learning histories, they may be suspicious of our findings. All the more reason for us to be specific in recognizing potential. A child may show great promise in voice, language, or content yet feel that it was accidental, a fluke; worse, she may not have a remote idea about how to achieve the same results again. This is where the teacher's questions, which confirm how the child did something, are important.

ACTION: **HELP CHILDREN REALIZE THEIR POTENTIAL AS LEARNERS OF WRITING.**

Try this. When children get something right, or show you a narrative, or solve any problem, no matter how small, ask them how they figured it out. I first confirm, then question:

- I see you put the period in just the right place; how did you figure that out?
- You caught a brown trout? How do you know how to do that? Is it hard?
- That last line; it catches me, makes me think. How did you come up with that?

ACTION: **DELIBERATELY LOOK AT CHILDREN WHO SEEM TO HAVE LOW POTENTIAL.**

Some children are irritating. Pointing out their potential to them is close to an emotional sellout. David was one of these children—a grasshopper, seldom able to concentrate for more than three minutes at a time; worse, he was intelligent enough to know all my emotional buttons. Yet he struggled with everything. His handwriting revealed all too clearly his emotional outbursts and the precarious nature of his learning. I'd go home after a day of teaching feeling defeated because things hadn't gone well with David. Thirty other students might have done well, but if David did poorly, I couldn't get him out of my mind. I was angry at David and probably angry at myself. Neither of us was able to function at our full potential.

That was many years ago, and I can't follow up with a success story to show that I recovered my balance as a professional and that David went on to better things. Even today I know that in my classes at the university there are some students with whom I find it difficult to work. It takes effort, tough observation, and a deliberate search for specific achievement in speech or in writing. The more I work at it, the more the potential of both of us is revealed. And I know that if I don't work on those tough cases, all my teaching is called into question.

Share your tough cases with other teachers, especially the person who may be trying the Actions in this book with you. This sharing may begin with complaints but ought to end up with a careful examination of what the child knows of skills, topics, and stories not yet written. When you talk with other professionals you should be prepared to point out:

- What stories the child could probably tell from his shortened draft.
- What skills the child already possesses.
- What learning history you've elicited from the child ("I see you've got that period in just the right place; how did you figure that out?").

Again, all of these should be considered without making any judgment, for or against.

ACTION:　　BE SELECTIVE IN SHARING A STUDENT'S POTENTIAL.

I remember the day I called a graduate student into my office to tell her what a good writer she was. I pointed out six or seven things she did rather well. I suggested that she had real talent as a writer. (And she did, because she published a number of articles several years later.) But she told me frankly that my revelation had been a curse. The burden of living up to that much potential was overwhelming. In retrospect, I think I should have been more judicious, pointing out one or two areas where she demonstrated particular ability and then offering specific help with those abilities.

FINAL REFLECTION All learners, teachers or students, need to be aware of their potential for learning, writing, and thinking. We all need to have the sense that our thoughts, our abilities, our skills can be put to work to communicate what is important to us. The more I reveal a student's potential, the more I discover my own potential as a teacher. They are inseparable. For this reason, we need to share *learning stories* within the classroom community: "This is what I learned and this is how I learned it." A sense of potential is the foundation upon which teachers and children can raise expectations for each other. The more we know *what* we know, the more we can challenge ourselves, direct our energies, and work with renewed intensity. The more we look for a child's potential, the more we can enjoy teaching, because we see real progress at the very points we have identified.

raise expectations

An expectation should be seen as an affirmation. When I expect something of myself, when I plan to undertake a new project, I should view it as self-affirmation. When I decide to teach a new course, write an article, or visit a friend whom I feel guilty about not having seen for some time, it is an act of confidence. I can *do* these things. Perhaps I unconsciously look over my history as a learner and say, "I can probably handle that."

Not all decisions are confident ones. I remember the day I decided to pursue a doctorate. The decision was more one of terror than self-affirmation. As a senior in college I was on academic probation; surely that kind of history doesn't give rise to a decision to enter into three years of study with a family of five children to support. Although the probation had occurred twenty years before and in the interim I'd pursued three other careers, the scars were strong enough to make my application more like a risky leap than a vote of personal confidence in myself. Yet even the greatest risk-taking is an expression of confidence. The head moves; the stomach reacts. Don't mistake the stomach's reaction for lack of confidence. The stomach is the brake, the censor for the head's action.

My decision wasn't made in a vacuum. In the intervening years I had been a school principal, a minister, and Director of Reading, Language, and Special Programs for a small city. That's the head part. And the head was right—and reasonably confident in spite of the academic problems.

When I notice that a child has used a good selection of information in handling a narrative sequence, I may say, "I think you are ready for some fiction now. Just the way you chose to elaborate here on this action shows that you ought to try some fiction. In fact, try writing *this* as fiction. Take half an hour and see what happens." I hope my saying this will help the child see that I have enough confidence in her to challenge her further. My suggestion is a vote of confidence. The child should begin to see within herself the possibility of good fiction writing.

147

I want children to recognize my expectations as a belief in their ability. Of course, this is not always possible. Because we stand outside the child, it is sometimes hard for her to perceive her own potential from our vantage point. It is too easy, however, to teach only at the point of a child's perception of her abilities. If I tune in too closely to the child's conscious perception of herself, I would consider it a drawback in my teaching.

Good teaching looks at Vygotsky's "zone of proximal development," where a sensitive teacher sees the possibility of new perceptions and nudges, recommends, and sometimes even expects immediate action. The zone of proximal development should become a zone of high expectations. As teachers, our expectations are high only when our own literacy is high. It is difficult to expect from children what we ourselves will not perceive and practice. This is why our own reading, writing, and engagement with the world are so important.

As we saw in Chapter 8, where I talked about potential, we will raise our expectations of ourselves along with those we have of children. This chapter seeks to act on our potential by helping children to act on theirs. It will consider how to extend what they are already doing and direct them into new experiences, new topics and genres, new skills and tools of the writer's craft.

Expectations change as the school year progresses. At the beginning of the year I generally listen longer in conferences than I do in May. In September I listen and question, question and listen. I want the child to hear his language and the growing authority in his own voice. I work hard so that both the child and I discover a sense of potential—and a sense of the possibilities ahead for us both. I confirm and I nudge: "Why don't you take a few minutes and cast that scene again, just the way you did when you told me a few minutes ago?" I particularly try to point out specific aspects of a child's learning history so that the child can make more specific plans. Since I've worked hard on the structure of the room (Chapter 3) and try to help children see the purpose and uniqueness of writing and reading (Chapters 4 and 5), I want all the children in the class to learn how to confirm each other's learning history as much as I do, perhaps more.

It's an incremental process: the stronger the learning history, the more plans the child has; the more plans, the more options the child can choose from; the more options, the more we can raise our expectations for each other. Conferences become shorter and more candid as the year advances. By May, they may simply end with: "Well, which ending are you going to try? Which will work best? I think it's time to choose, don't you?"

Our sense of expectation should not be directed entirely at individuals. We should also consider the classroom as a whole. I work very hard to help a class have a sense of history and a sense of community: "Together we can do these things. We have these plans. This is what we will do to achieve them." The community should be greater than the sum of all the individuals in the classroom.

The Actions in this chapter focus on experiments with individuals and with the group. In one sense, this chapter may be the most difficult as we move from contemplating potential in individual children and in ourselves to deliberately challenging children to explore new ground. The risks are higher, but the rewards are greater.

ACTION: FIND A CHILD WITH PLANS.

Start with children who already have plans and expectations for themselves:

- A child in the middle of a piece who knows what she will write next.
- A child who knows what his next topic will be.

- A child who plans to publish the next piece.
- A child who wants to learn a particular skill.
- A child looking for a particular author or new book.

I expect children to follow through on their plans. In my first conference, I take a child at his word. If he says he knows his next topic, I make it a point to come back to see how his plans are working out. If he has abandoned his topic, I want to know why. I listen carefully to his reasons; they may be good ones. On the other hand, some help may improve the situation; I demonstrate a solution, see if the child understands, and then leave him to try the offered solution. My whole tone shows my confidence that he has the power to produce good thinking. Sometimes we celebrate. Celebration recognizes a particular success while suggesting that greater possibilities are just around the corner.

Some of the children's plans may not work. When problems arise I examine those areas that both the child and I control.

ACTION: SHARE YOUR OWN PLANS AND HOW YOU CHALLENGE YOURSELF.

Teachers in my research course frequently say, "When I told my students about my research topic, they all pitched in to help. They kept telling me things that helped my teaching." Even if the teacher doesn't share the particulars about her research the fact that a she is doing research inspires children to state their views and perceptions. The mood of the room changes. Linda Rief of Oyster River Middle School in Durham, New Hampshire, came up with the research question "What happens if children are the primary source of evaluation in the classroom?" This meant that she had to ask children regularly for their evaluations of their work. They became so practiced in evaluating for themselves that they developed more independence, and the quality of their writing greatly improved.

We need to share our plans with children so that they can participate. We need to demonstrate how we plan and challenge ourselves. Children will begin to understand the nature of self-challenge if they can participate with us. Here are some examples of the kinds of shared challenges I address to the class:

- "I'm going to try to work on the specifics in my own writing. I'd like you to respond."
- "I'd like to come up with a better way to publish or rethink all the ways we might consider something published."
- "I keep getting distracted in conferences. I want to listen more effectively. I'm going to work on that. Have you got any ideas about how we can make conferences work more effectively?"
- "This is a complicated one. I'd like to see if some of you could figure out what kind of information books we ought to have in this room. But since we don't have any money to buy books, once we discover what we need maybe some of you would take on the challenge of writing them. What do you think?"

Sharing plans and challenges is a consistent, natural outgrowth of the writing/reading conference. Children should be used to teaching us about what they know in conference. Sharing plans is merely an extension of the collaboration that already exists in the conference. Children want to help; they want to know about how we continue to learn. Include them in the process and a community grows; exclude them and we all lose a valuable source of wisdom and supportive energy.

Let me be clear. I am not speaking of the situation in which a teacher bares her professional soul: "I wish the other teachers in this building would respect me more. I want to work on that." Or "My challenge is to go on and get a doctorate."

Rather, I mean a collaborative situation in which children can see a way to help that is within their reach.

The challenge you share may not be stated specifically enough: "I wish we had a better feeling in this room." Here, it would be better to say, "I'd like to work toward better listening. For three days running I've noticed that during sharing time people seem to be thinking of other things. It doesn't seem as though the author sharing his piece gets a good hearing. Remember Bill's piece this morning? How can we improve the situation?"

ACTION: DEMONSTRATE A CHALLENGE WITHIN A PIECE OF WRITING.

Children need to see us spot a challenge *within* a piece of writing. As you compose a piece, be open to changes, discoveries, and new genres. I'll compose a short piece here to show you what I mean and then talk aloud about changes:

About this time of year the mice start to invade our home. That's the way it is in New Hampshire in February. My wife just popped in to say, "I've noticed that the mice are having a good time with your bag of sunflower seeds in the basement." I have sunflower seeds to feed birds, not mice.

DON [*to class*]: Now look at that. I didn't expect to find birds and mice on the same line. It just struck me that I like the idea of feeding birds but I don't like it when mice come in to take what I have for the birds. But the mice need to be fed, too. After all, mice can have as much of a problem with food in winter as the birds. What should I be thinking about right now? What are you thinking about?

The minute I wonder, "How come?," I listen to myself answer, and the act of listening makes me stop, perhaps to write in another direction, determine what I'll write next, or say, "I'll come back to that later." What is important here is that I demonstrate listening to the text, talking aloud, and showing the challenge a text gives me. As I continue to write, I respond to the issue of mice and birds:

> *I've never been sympathetic to mice until now. There are all kinds of books like* Anatole, Three Mice, *and others that ought to make me think of a way to care for the mice. These are deer mice with brown fur, white bellies, and big floppy ears, just like the mice that Walt Disney chooses for his cartoons.*
>
> *But wait a minute. How come there aren't any societies to protect mice? There's the Audubon Society to protect birds. How come I go to the hardware store and see traps that will get rid of mice?*

DON [*to class*]: I've got to stop here and do some reading. I know it makes things go more slowly, but I have plenty of time. There's a big question that keeps popping up inside me. Here it is: "Birds are really important for keeping down insects and carrying seeds to make things grow everywhere. I wonder if mice do anything beneficial for the world. How can we find out?"

In this example, I'm demonstrating that questions continually arise. I may deal with a question on the spot in the text, or I may write it on a piece of paper so that I won't forget it and then go on. The main point of all this demonstrating is that I *show* how I deal with challenges. I *show* that challenges are exciting. I *show* how I handle the process and how I use time.

We need to be careful not to introduce too many options in a demonstration. In this demonstration I've tried to deal with only one: "Why should I feed birds and not mice?" We also need to be careful not to present six ways of dealing with a question, thinking that more options will provide a broad base for problem solving and include more children. Unfortunately, it usually doesn't work that way. Too many options can produce overload and mental confusion. Children won't be able to integrate what is new with what they already know.

If children think they must demonstrate what I have done immediately, the shared piece will produce regressive learning. My timing can't be good enough to address where each is in a particular piece. But what I want to do is set a tone of personal challenge and inspire a sense of inquiry that will be useful for both of us to refer to in our conferences.

ACTION: HELP CHILDREN SHARE PERSONAL CHALLENGES FROM THEIR OWN READING.

Personal challenges are usually shared within small groups. The groups I refer to are the mixed ability groups of readers who meet daily to share their reading and current experiences with books. Several times a week, ask the children to share the challenges they have recently undertaken to improve themselves as readers. Here are some possibilities:

- "I'm trying this book on sharks. It is hard to read but I think I can get quite a lot from the pictures, the words I know, and some help from Ricky."
- "I'm going to read all the Ramona books."
- "I can't seem to finish my books and I *am* going to finish this one."
- "I'm making a list of hard reading words I want to know."
- "The letters I write about my books are too short; I want them to be longer." (In this class the children write letters to the teacher and to other children in the class about the books they are reading, and teachers and children write back. See Graves 1990, Chapter 4.)
- "There's this character in my book I like and I'd like to make a character like him in my story."
- "I'd like to know a way to read faster." (One child said, "If things are really hard I just read all the talking parts.")

ACTION: PRACTICE RECOMMENDATIONS.

Recommendations are based on timely observations—for example, that a child needs to "get wet" trying something new. You will need a full repertoire of responses, from allowing children to exercise full choice through negotiation to the opposite pole: "No choice. Do this now!" Good teachers have always cultivated this repertoire, especially if their children are taking more and more responsibility for their own learning. Your aim is to recommend that a child move into something new based on what that child is already doing—to extend the child's choice and action into the "zone of proximal development," the potential zone of learning. If you spot a child writing a piece of fiction, here is a sample and recommendations that *might* result:

The good gys beat the bad gys. The good gys was winn the war cz thay had lazr n the bad gys ran awa.

TEACHER: Jonathan, would you read this piece to me? [*I also observe the content in his drawings as he reads, putting together his voice in the text and in the drawing. The more I know about his "voice," the more I may be able to recommend.*]

JONATHAN: [*Reads piece, seems to be involved as he points to the "good guys" with their lasers.*]

TEACHER: I see that the good guys are winning because they have these lasers, Jonathan. Who are these good guys? I don't know much about them.

JONATHAN: Oh, they made the lasers. They're experts.

TEACHER [*knowing there is a point where the action and the tools are more important than the agents—people—the teacher seeks to extend to see where Jonathan is*]: What can you call these good guys so we won't forget who has the lasers?

JONATHAN: The laser people.

TEACHER: Ah, now I'll know. How can you show it so I won't forget?

[*Jonathan puts "LP" on the front of the laser people in his drawings.*]

Many other recommendations could have been made about Jonathan's piece. The question "Who are those people?" moved him from action and tools to characters. Adding dimension to characters often begins with their names. The "bad guys" haven't been named yet, but the notion of using names for people has been established. Following the conference you'd use the name "laser people" to establish the usefulness of the name and help it take root. It might be argued that Jonathan should have identified the characters in his text instead of in his drawing. At this point, however, his drawing is far more significant than his writing. It contains more information than the text.

Some recommendations sound more like directives and probably are. As the year advances and teacher and student have a more candid level of exchange, I'll say things like:

- You have the beginning of a poem here. Listen. [*I read it.*] Before the morning is out take another sheet and see what happens.
- That upsets you, doesn't it? Take ten minutes and write what you feel as fast as you can.
- I think you need quiet time. Why not go to the quiet area where you can think without interruption?

Most of the time, if my observations are right and the timing is good, the child will take the recommendation. If there are issues I don't understand, we can negotiate. There are also times when a recommendation can change to a directive: "Finish the poem, Margaret."

In our last research project at Stratham Memorial School in Stratham, New Hampshire, teachers and children exchanged letters about the books each was reading. Within the letters the teachers raised the level of challenge for the children as well as for themselves, most frequently through recommendations:

- "You'd love *Matilda* by Roald Dahl. You want to borrow it next?" [*child to teacher*]
- "If you like S. E. Hinton, try *The Outsiders*." [*teacher to child*]
- "Sarah, for some reason you aren't finishing your books lately. What's the story? Let's talk." [*teacher to child*]

In reviewing the quality of the letters as part of the research study, we found that the level of challenge teachers gave themselves in their letters was an important counterpoint to the challenge they directed at their students.

ACTION: PRACTICE DIRECTIVES.

Be conscious of those occasions when you use directives. The more choices children have, the more they need to understand the limits of their choices. Choice without limits places children in one of the most difficult behavioral prisons. Children in classrooms without limits inevitably push for the edge, for the limits, so they can discover the comfort of the boundary.

Some children live in homes where there are few boundaries, or at least where the boundaries are set well beyond those a teacher would ordinarily set. Furthermore, these children may be used to testing any boundaries that may be explicitly set.

I've observed children come into Pat McLure's first-grade classroom at Mast Way School on the first day of school and be at work in three or four areas after a short class meeting on the rug. She focuses on what children can do; the doors to opportunity are open. She sets limits quietly and individually for those few children who do not understand the tasks at hand. But the limits are firm and usually in the form of recommendations, which move to recommendations without choice and sometimes to an occasional final directive: "No, you must finish this work before you go on." "No, that is Daniel's. This is yours."

If the edges of possibility are too confined and the choices available too unchallenging or too poorly thought out, children will test the limits, and you will find directives popping out of your mouth every two minutes. That is a time for rethinking the task.

On the other hand, it is important for you to have the directive, the limiting move, clearly in hand. It should be part of your repertoire as a professional. Teachers continually ask me, "Do you ever tell the child to do something?"

"Heavens, yes!" I respond. After a while I realize why teachers ask. We emphasize listening and helping children to speak their minds, and to find their voices. Not many of our examples show us directing the child to get moving.

I'd stress that a voice is also found within limits. Laissez-faire writing and reading with no heat under it can lead to an unchanging, homeostatic learner. We have opinions and feelings, and we assign limits to ourselves—or do we? Ask yourself what you've said no to lately and you'll find out whether you are a person who can help others set limits. As in all our other actions, practice on yourself as well as on others.

A youngster once wrote a rather nasty piece in Nancie Atwell's class about a frivolous Saturday night. Nancie quickly diagnosed the piece as pandering to the group rather than being an honest statement about an event. Her simple response was "I find that offensive. Is it something appropriate to be writing in school?" After the initial shock, the student probably felt relieved to run into some limits.

Directives can be used positively. I'll use a child's own language in a piece to show what strikes me. The tone is positive and one of learning on my part. Occasionally, however, a child will make a major breakthrough and be unaware of it. I'll be specific in my response yet declare simultaneously, "That's the best piece I've seen you do this year, and here's why."

The reason praise works in this instance is that it is used sparingly. Sadly, I see an abundance of praise in classrooms, most of it manipulative. Too often, teachers use praise to get the child to do the next small step. For every little step the child gets the verbal equivalent of an M&M, a candied phrase of encouragement: "Good job. Nice talking. You are on your way." But the subtle message to the child is "You are on my track." Worse, it implies that the teacher is the only one who can tell the child she is doing well. She is unable to decide for herself.

Praise can be a substitute for specific professional observation. Rather than saying, "I like your piece," I'd say, "When I close my eyes and hear those words I can see the crooked smile on Walter's face when he knew he wasn't telling the truth." In this way, I demonstrate the power of the child's words. I don't need to tell him the description is good. The child can decide for himself.

Sometimes I use directives to rescue writers from their own problems. If I see a child's piece losing altitude from too much drafting, I simply say, "The piece is due tomorrow." I once watched a fourth-grade teacher tell a child who couldn't put paper to pencil after he came up with a good plan for the piece, "I'll be back in ten minutes and I want this page half-filled." The page was soon half-filled with an excellent text. The teacher tried the same tactic several weeks later with another child; it didn't work, because she had misjudged the child's ability to write about the subject.

I also use directives in reading. "Your book choices aren't working. This week I'll choose one of your books and you can choose two. You need to choose one book that's a little easier. Here's how."

Directives and strong suggestions are much more difficult with some children than others. Here are a few types.

Tom   Tom is an intelligent, verbal child, but he is simply not used to initiating activity. His home pattern is one of dependence, a carefully fostered dependence, where he either has chores done for him or receives a constant reminder that he ought to get going. Tom waits out directives until things get hot enough for him to act or the other person gives up in despair or does the task for him. Tom has a disarming, shy type of smile that gives you the impression of a pleasant geniality, that he misunderstood a directive or that it will soon be done. It doesn't get done.

Tom is the kind of child who will quickly move us into the same pattern as his mother: constant directives. His delaying power is aided by the camouflage of a classroom of 24 to 26 other children. He is adept at becoming part of the woodwork.

Help for Tom and myself comes from a carefully constructed classroom community where children have many different kinds of responsibilities at different times of the day. If Tom's initiative is only exercised during writing, then both of us are trapped. On the other hand, in a classroom community where some chores are teamed, where children help each other and other children have the chance to respond to Tom as well as ourselves, then Tom's initiative problem falls into a more broadly based framework.

My timing is also selective. I direct or push at the points of Tom's strengths, a topic he knows and cares about, or a point where Tom has a good understanding of what he will write next. I work hard to review Tom's writing folder with him, to develop a history of what he knows and a history of initiative; I try to team him up to help new persons in the room.

Directives and strong suggestions work well in a decentralized room where children are expected to exercise their own judgment and self-evaluative powers. In a centralized room where the teacher starts and stops all activity and children move and talk by permission only, directives or suggestions are scarcely heard. In a community of learners, where helping and mutual listening are commonplace, a directive is a moment for action.

Kristen Kristen works slowly, struggles to find her way, and is very cautious about venturing out into the proximal zone. Her progress is glacial and although I usually give her plenty of room to go at her own pace, I have the feeling that a few strong suggestions would help her to explore more new ground and develop a better picture of herself as a risk taker.

I need to experiment consciously with both Tom and Kristen. I need to remind myself that a directive is an affirmation that "you can do it." Children are not destroyed by high expectations. I expect, watch, expect again, or back off. But above all, I expect. I listen very carefully to children's plans, which arise from their learning histories. Children like Kristen often proceed so slowly in their development that their own personal histories as learners are lost to them. When Kristen accomplishes something, even something as small as putting a period in the right place, I say, "You got that in the right place. How did you figure that out?" Kristen may have no recollection, but she may be able to come up with a reason or even invent one to build on her fragile history as a learner.

FINAL REFLECTION Your work on "expectations" began when you chose to try some of the experiments in this book. You had expectations for yourself when you wrote with your children, practiced listening to your own voice, and began to delegate more responsibility to the children.

It is equally important to have a high enough regard for

children that you expect still more of them than they may currently think is possible for themselves. We listen carefully to the children, allow them to hear their own voices, then confirm what they may not realize they are expressing. In this way, they can begin to build a rich learning history. A large proportion of our challenges and recommendations must come in that context. Otherwise, we may sound as if we think children have no expectations for themselves; they will come to rely on us as the single driving force for their learning.

Within the broad framework of a classroom in which children take responsibility and help each other, challenge is welcome. We need to see that risk taking is a necessary part of their intellectual diet. If we see learning strictly as work, they will too. We have yet to see what children can really do in the face of an intelligent, literate challenge.

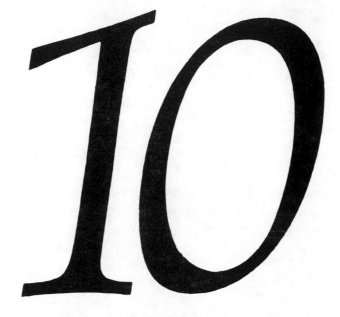

10

evaluate your own classroom

Tests are not going to go away. They are a fact of educational life. Until teachers themselves take assessment into their own hands, require a more demanding evaluation than that provided in standardized tests, and begin to ask more penetrating questions of those who ordain such testing, literacy will continue to be defined in terms of failure. Tests define what kind of literacy is acceptable.

Current assessment approaches simply can't identify the children who demonstrate the new kind of literacy produced by the classrooms I have described in this book. Tests cannot identify which children will become lifelong readers, nor can they predict those who will initiate writing for themselves or sustain reading and writing over several days or weeks to acquire a deeper understanding of the world around them. The tests do identify children who can handle the "five-meter sprint" of reading several paragraphs and answering the questions underneath the text. What is worse, the major responsibility for assessment is delegated to unknown people out of town, who design, score, and pass on the graphs and charts about individual, class, school, and system placement in relation to the nation as a whole. The wisdom of those closest to the learning operation itself is bypassed in the guise of objectivity.

Teachers, in league with universities and their own professional organizations, need to provide more effective approaches to alternative assessment. This chapter is intended to help you examine the significant elements that affect the quality of literacy in your classroom. The Actions in this book have already pointed you in a direction for evaluating your own classroom. This chapter will provide a little more detail in helping you with a data base in which you can help children to take more responsibility for evaluation, redirect your own teaching, as well as assist your challenge to less effective forms of evaluating. The Actions will first help you to review the large, fundamental questions that deal with the use of literacy and then move gently and specifically to more detailed information. Evaluation of your own literacy will be fundamental to the children's participation in the process of evaluating their own progress in reading, writing, and thinking.

ACTION: REVIEW YOUR OWN PERSONAL PRACTICES IN READING AND WRITING.

Evaluation begins with your own practices. Begin with yourself because it is your own spirit of inquiry, your own investigation of the world around you through books and writing that affects the literate life of your children. Review the following questions:

• What books were you "lost" in within the last six months? These were books that you simply couldn't put down because you became absorbed in the author's way of presenting information.

• Did you read the daily newspaper four out of the last seven days? What are the top three news stories from your town, state, nation, the world? What are your predictions about their outcomes? What is your place in these predictions? With whom did you discuss the news?

• What are the three or four life questions that consistently run through your mind? These are questions that relate to life, death, purpose, existence, and so forth. What do they move you to do? Read? Write?

• What have you written in the last six months that represented writing to "find out"? That is, you encountered a complex event and you wrote to find out what something meant. These are usually short occasional pieces. They are often written with the children in the classroom. Perhaps you tried some poetry or fiction with the children.

• Have you listened to a tape-recording of your work with the children in reading, writing, or learning conferences?

Listen for the balance between the amount of time you talk and the children talk. Listen to yourself as a learner with the children. Listen to yourself using a child's information to learn more and to *expect* more of that child.

• What new thing, practice, or process have you learned in the last six months? This should have no direct connection with school, but is something you learned out of your own curiosity.

For more on this, see *Discover Your Own Literacy* (Graves 1990).

ACTION: SPOT THE LIFELONG READER/WRITER.

I begin with an examination of the greatest question in my own evaluation scheme: Can I spot the lifelong reader/writer? That is, can I say with some assurance that a particular child in my classroom will choose to read and write independently for the rest of his or her life? After all, I work with my children not so that they may pass a test, achieve good grades, or even read a book to please me. Since I will only have one year to work with these children, I focus on my role in contributing to their life-time habits as readers and writers. I want them to see that books are essential to their lives today and to exercise initiative in reading because they are confident that books serve their interests now. I look for these signs in reading:

• Reads at least three complete books per month (provided there is adequate time in class to read).
• Identifies "favorite" authors.
• Initiates reading to locate information.
• Shares reading with others, initiates sharing.

And these in writing:

• Chooses topics easily.
• Has a strong sense of audience.
• Initiates the sharing of his work.

- Writes in at least three genres.
- Writes in order to find out what she means.
- Uses writing as a means to learn.

Notice how often I use the word *initiate*. When children initiate learning today, I know they will be more likely to initiate reading and writing for themselves when they are adults. This does not mean (as Chapter 9 attests) that I do not make strong recommendations and give downright blunt, no-nonsense directives to children.

ACTION: ESTABLISH PORTFOLIOS AS A MEANS FOR MORE EFFECTIVE, CONTINUOUS EVALUATION.

The use of portfolios offers one of the most promising opportunities for evaluating children's development in reading and writing that I have seen in some time. Portfolios were common in several fields long before we considered them in education. Artists use them to demonstrate both the range and the depth of their work. The artist works day by day, experimenting with various media and perhaps specializing in one area. Periodically, the artist selects material from the broader work for a portfolio to show to other artists, studios, or judges.

Portfolios comprise work taken from the more traditional folder, in which, in the past, all of the child's writing has been collected. Every six to eight weeks, the child reviews his folder looking for those pieces he might select to show his best work as well as any experiments he has attempted in order to extend and diversify his portfolio.

I maintain a folder and a portfolio in order to show children how I make decisions when I select material from my folder. Occasionally, I'll talk about how I experiment and try new things: "Today I'm going to try a poem. I need to experiment with new things to help my thinking. There was a crazy driver I saw on the way to school, and I think I'll try to handle what

I felt in a poem." Portfolios also provide an opportunity to display depth at the point of our strengths. I may choose personal narrative or poetry. Of course, at the beginning of the year I may not be aware of my depth area; I am still exploring. By mid-year, however, I should see the material in my portfolio broaden and deepen.

Children in the primary years maintain shorter-term portfolios. Eight weeks to a first grader may be the equivalent of a year to an older student. You will need to experiment, since children's understanding of time and choice varies enormously among them at any grade level. The portfolio provides opportunities for children's growth and an effective medium for continuing evaluation.

- Children actively participate in the evaluation process by selecting the "best" three papers they have written in an eight-week period. It is also an opportunity for children to make the best better.
- Children become more aware of their experiments and their specialties. When children write in only one genre, the portfolio helps them to see where they might try experimenting and where they might work toward greater depth. Experimentation does not work, however, unless you are demonstrating how you experiment with new kinds of writing yourself.
- Portfolios are ideal for planning. When children realize that they need to broaden their writing, the portfolio is a means to plan future work.

Children review their portfolios every eight or nine weeks throughout the school year—or four or five times each year. Each time, they might add some new pieces and remove some old ones that they no longer consider their "best" work or that do not fit the kind of profile they wish their work to convey. By the end of the year, children should become more adept at evaluating their work. By this time, too, they should have a collection of writing of which they are proud.

You will find it helpful to have children share the ways in which they are experimenting with various topics and genres in both large and small group sessions. Children need to hear how other children make their evaluative decisions.

It is equally important for children to maintain a reading portfolio. (Since a portfolio contains only selected material, there should be adequate room for both reading and writing selections.) Reading portfolios are still in the experimental stage, and the debate about what should be included as evidence of reading activity continues.

Reading portfolios require a broader interpretation than writing portfolios. The objectives for reading portfolios are similar, to show both range and depth. But in the reading portfolio, the child will include favorite books, authors, and characters. It should also contain evidence that the child is experimenting with various kinds of reading in order to push his achievement toward new information and new thinking.

Some of the contents of the reading portfolio will most certainly be writing the child has done *about* her reading. Some of the letters mentioned in Chapter 5, "What Reading Does," can be selected to show significant books and moments in the child's reading. If teachers use reading journals, the child can select entries from the journal for the reading portfolio.

Although writing is an important way to express what is important, some children are penalized if writing is the sole means of reporting about their reading. The key element in the reading portfolio is the opportunity it affords the child to demonstrate good thinking about books, especially books that have had a significant impact in the child's life. Thus, an illustration or a carefully prepared oral reading of important scenes, with editorialized oral tapes or written comment, could be an important element in the child's reading portfolio.

The reading portfolio might also contain a written piece about a favorite author with background on the author's life. The child might even attempt to write a short piece that deliberately reflects the style of the author he enjoys. Lists—of characters, authors, book titles—are also appropriate for the reading portfolio, with a written reflection on the importance of the list for the child.

During children's extensive daily reading in trade books, they are constantly sifting and judging what strikes them as important evidence of their profile as readers. The portfolio contributes to my evaluation of the effectiveness of my literate classroom because it offers another, higher level of judgment. Children can say, "This is important; this is my best. I want this good work to be singled out from all that I have done as a significant piece or a significant moment in the year." Simply put, portfolios provide visibility so that children can make more refined evaluations. In addition, since I maintain a writing and reading portfolio myself, I learn new ways to demonstrate how the portfolio works.

You may find it difficult to keep reading and writing selections in separate portfolios. When literacy is working well it is indeed difficult to know where one ends and the other begins. Although you may begin with separate portfolios, know that the system is working *well* when children complain that they're not sure whether a piece represents reading or writing.

ACTION: HELP CHILDREN KEEP GOOD RECORDS.

Since children are the most important evaluators in the classroom, they need to learn how to keep effective records on their progress. A large amount of your effort in evaluating your classroom will be spent in helping children maintain records and in directing them to observe and evaluate their own progress.

But if children have to keep too many records, your system

won't work. The most important records are the collections in the folder and the portfolio. The folder contains all the child's work from the beginning of the year with the exception of those papers removed and put in the portfolio. Since reading and writing at the folder level can be quite voluminous, one folder usually needs to be kept for each. The cover of each folder contains a summary of what the child has read or written (see Figure 10–1).

In addition, I still like to have children maintain records of the skills or conventions they learn on the inside cover of their reading and writing folders. Children should be aware of the repertoire of conventions they are learning and the source of their learning. They record the title of the piece and the approximate place where they used it successfully (see Figure 10–2). In this way, children build their own reference book to consult for help in using conventions.

Another type of useful kind of information is the child's own plans for learning (see Figure 10–3). In a section on the inside of the folder, the child records what she wants to learn over the next six to eight weeks. The period is shorter for younger children.

Some children have a difficult time keeping records. I've observed a number of problems like these:

- "I know what I'm doing." This child has a strong sense of what he is doing and can't see the sense in maintaining records. The time spent in keeping records could better be spent in reading or writing.
- "It's hopeless." This child doesn't want to keep records because her work habits are poor. Her writing is incomplete and there are few papers in the folder; she seldom finishes books. She keeps losing her work. For this child, a record is only further documentation of failure.
- "What does it mean?" For this child the record stands for

FIGURE 10–1   FOLDER COVERS. A: WRITING. B: READING.

Date Started	Genre	Piece Publish = P	Date finished or dropped
9/9	Fiction	The Avengers	9/14 F
9/17	Fiction	The Avengers Return	9/23 F
9/26	Personal narr.	My Dog	9/28 F
9/29	Letter	Wrote with Justin to the principal	10/3 F

A

Date Started	Genre	Book	Date finished or dropped
9/12	Fiction Adventure	—maybe history? The Black Cauldron	9/22 F
9/25	Info-Science	The Magic School Bus	9/26 F
9/28	Fiction	Stuart Little	10/2 F
10/4	Fiction	The Trumpet of the Swan	10/8 F
10/9	?	The Desert Is Theirs	10/9 D

B

FIGURE 10–2   RECORD OF CONVENTIONS

Convention	Date	Page	Piece
comma (serial)	10/2	1	Dog to the Vet
colon	10/30	2	Whales
cap-name	11/6	1	Trip to New York
apostrophe (contraction)	11/21	3	Space Story

FIGURE 10–3   RECORD OF PLANS

Date		Check if accomplished
9/15	Read Lloyd Alexander	✓
10/10	Proof better on my last drafts	
10/30	Publish my dog piece	✓
11/3	Learn quotations for speaking parts	
12/2	Ask better questions in book share	✓

little. It is an abstraction that doesn't represent to him the work accomplished.

Unless children use the records they keep, record keeping makes little sense. I schedule small sessions in which children look over their records and tell me the story of their progress. The most difficult child to help is the child who has not accomplished much. The "it's hopeless" child needs to know, more than any other child in the room, what progress she has made. For this child, I spend more time searching for change and confirming that change has occurred. And I make sure the progress is recorded and shared with others where feasible.

ACTION: EVALUATE CHILDREN'S ABILITY TO EVALUATE THEIR OWN WORK.

As I have noted, the child is the most important evaluator in the entire chain of evaluation that leads from child to teacher, principal, system, state, and national exam. If the child plays no major role in the scheme, then the system fails. Children spend 99 percent of their time with a book or a written piece. If they are not schooled in self-evaluation, the entire evaluation system is incomplete. There are several ways in which I review a child's ability to self-evaluate:

- Docs the child maintain effective records?
- Can the child articulate progress?
- Are the child's plans realistic and built upon past learning?
- How well does the child sense what reading and writing are for? (See Chapters 4 and 5.)
- How much is the child dependent on others (particularly you, the teacher) for confirmation of progress?

ACTION: ESTABLISH THE INVERTED PYRAMID APPROACH TO EVALUATION.

The pyramid approach to evaluating class progress is based on a differentiated review of children's literacy. Some children need a more detailed review than others, and the pyramid reflects that approach. Figure 10–4 shows a pyramid with three levels of review. In Level 1, I review data on all the children and choose several key variables to examine in each child. Some examples of data I might choose to review at this level are the following:

- How wide a range of books is the class reading?
- How broad are the genres the children choose in their writing?
- Who are the authors the children read most? least?
- What common patterns do I see in the children's plans?

Data for the first three questions can be handled by the children with the use of a calculator. They are based on summaries of the records the children have kept themselves. The fourth question I will do myself, since I will use it to plan mini-lessons.

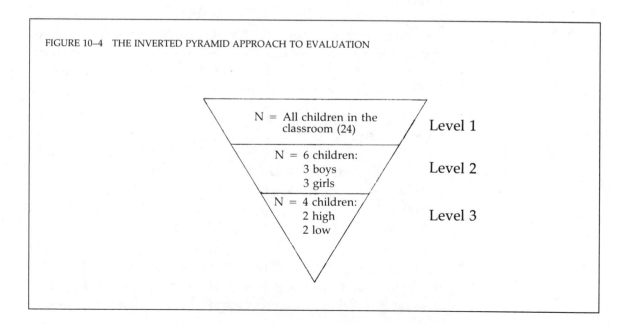

FIGURE 10–4 THE INVERTED PYRAMID APPROACH TO EVALUATION

Level 2 requires more detailed evaluation. In a class of twenty-four I choose six children based on information gathered in Level 1: one boy and one girl from low, middle, and high achievement levels. The detailed work in this section of the pyramid makes me aware of the progress of these six children, but it also sensitizes me to the progress of other children in the classroom.

I read selections from the children's fiction writing and from the letters they write me about the fiction they are reading. In both the reading and writing I look for changes in the following in order to note children's growth:

- Ability to talk about reading and writing.
- Ability to have plots evolve from the nature of characters in their fiction.
- Ability to attend to the relationship between character and plot in reading.
- Ability to sense authorship in letters written about the books they read. In short, does the child understand that a person is behind the writing in the book? Does the child sense what options the author had in writing the book?
- Ability to sense that you also read and react to books. Does the child ask you questions about your books or make statements to you about reading?
- Ability to represent other points of view in letters and essays.

Literacy depends a great deal on our ability to understand the world of our fellow humans, their points of view, motives, and foibles. So I examine these critical variables in children's texts. (To understand how children change in these important abilities, see Chapter 6 in *Experiment with Fiction*, which traces children's use of fiction from the first through the sixth grades and "When Children Respond to Fiction" in *Language Arts*, October

1989. The development of children's sense of point of view is discussed in *Investigate Nonfiction*.)

Level 3 requires still more detailed analysis. I look at the following types of children in this section:

- High potential: I choose two children who read and write well yet do not seem to have much sense of purpose in their work. Their level of self-challenge is low.
- Low performance: I choose two children who I sense do not thrive on the kind of environment I have established in my classroom. Such elements as responsibility, self-direction, choice of activity, or the effective use of time seem foreign to them. They want to be told what to do, fear new problems, and constantly ask if what they are doing is correct. At the same time, children in this category may simply be quiet, do nothing, drift, and be quite adept at not being noticed. They slip by much more easily than unruly children or those who blatantly challenge your kind of classroom.

I use all the data sources from Level 2 to examine these children, since any changes in their understanding of character or their use of reading and writing will be important. I look especially for what their interests are and the types of plans they express in their folders as well as their sense of their own history as learners. Then I examine what kind of challenge I am giving them (see Chapter 9 for further detail). Above all, I want to listen to these children tell me about their perception of the situation.

When I review children in Level 3, I consult with a colleague and help her likewise in reviewing children in her classroom. We do this because we are often blind to the strengths and weaknesses of the children we see every day and to the solutions that will help them. We look for specific information about the risks they are taking and the risks they ought to be taking.

ACTION: EVALUATE CHILDREN'S WORK WITH CONVENTIONS.

By now you should be aware that you are using time differently when you assess children's progress. No longer are you spending hours correcting sheaves of papers. You are working just as hard, probably harder, but now you are making sure that children keep track of their progress and practice evaluating their own work. You take folders and portfolios home on a scheduled basis but not to correct. Now you look through them to help you plan mini-lessons and schedule your time. You study them for ways to give children more responsibility and check on the fulfillment of their plans.

I try to link my informal assessment of children's proficiency in conventions with my mini-lessons. I ask myself, "Do children expand their repertoire of conventions as I demonstrate them in mini-lessons?" I am curious about what conventions seem to stick, since I recognize that some are more difficult to acquire than others. As I noted earlier, where to put commas in a series is much easier for young children to learn than where to put a period.

I also keep track of children's knowledge of sound/symbol relationships. There has been much debate about teaching children phonics as an essential skill in learning to read. Although the evidence shows that children can learn to read a word from context, the use of pictures, the sight sense of the word, and so on, when they write, they do need to know what letters represent the sounds they hear in a word. They remember some words more easily, especially those of high frequency in the culture or those that produce strong visual imagery, like *kiss*, *elephant*, or *stegosaurus*.

Mary Ellen Giacobbe (1981) devised a twenty-word spelling list she administers to her first-grade children three times during the year—September, January, and June. Even though many of the children cannot spell words when they enter in September, she still asks them to try to write these words as a baseline to their growing ability to know sound/letter combinations. The list could be used with older children as well. The progress of six children in learning to spell is shown in Figure 10–5 in their September and June spellings of ten of the twenty words. The top word in the box is the September spelling and the bottom word, the June spelling. The ten words not represented here are:

camp	zero	hill	tack	five
pickle	muffin	wife	job	quick

Poor spellers often find it difficult to sense progress in their ability to spell words. They know instinctively that a heavy percentage of the words they write are misspelled. This is especially true if they try to approximate spellings with their own inventions rather than choose other words they know they can spell. These children rarely look back at the impossible task of identifying and correcting misspellings.

Effective self-assessment for these children begins with learning how to make an informed guess. That is, a poor speller returns to his writing to sense what words may be misspelled. Ask that same child to keep records of his growing ability to tell which words may be misspelled. (The same can be done with punctuation and many other tasks in science and mathematics.) Children simply need to practice.

ACTION: **TAKE A HARD LOOK AT STANDARDIZED TESTS.**

Most districts mandate standardized tests. States, boards of education, and administrators require them. They are a fact of life in the United States, particularly in the last four years. Administrators and boards of education establish their reputations on their ability to "raise" scores. Reading, more than any other curriculum area, receives undue focus. Sadly, most of the work in standardized reading assessment resembles end-of-book tests or vice versa: several short paragraphs with ques-

FIGURE 10–5   SIX CHILDREN'S PROGRESS, SEPTEMBER–JUNE (FROM GRAVES 1983, P. 185)

	EC	HD	FG	CG	JG	AH
rag	rag Rag	ro rag	F Rat	Rag Rag	Rakg Rag	rog rag
buzz	Bozo Bas	B biz	P pls	Bis bis	Bas bas	das buss
lid	lad lid	lo led	L lah	lad lad	lid lid	lid lid
six	sax six	SE ses	S sak	sgs ses	sik si	six six
game	gam Gam	GM gam	G KAM	Gam Gam	GAM Gam	gam game
nice	nis nis	 Nis	N NS	Nas Nis	NAS Nis	nis nis
doctor	Dokr Dodr	D Dodr	D Drdkr	Dldi Dctor	DAODR Docdr	dodr docdr
view	vuog vyou	 vuy	 For	Equ Vou	Voo Vioo	vyoo Vyou
yellow	yolow yalow	ELO ualou	E ALO	Lol ilo	YALO Yaloo	yaloow yiey
kiss	kas kiss	KS ces	S kass	Kas cas	KES Kis	kiss kiss

tions 1 to 5 and answer slots A to E, to be filled in with a Number 2 pencil.

Most of the paragraphs on these tests are poorly written and voiceless. There is an uninspiring quality to the diction that is certainly less than a challenge to a mind that already cares little about reading. There is also little room for the reader to compose her own text or to come up with a new interpretation: the text has already been "set" for a single interpretation.

Make no mistake, I have to read texts written in this manner as part of my day-to-day life. If, in assembling my mother's new screened-in porch using directions written by some foreign manufacturer, I mistake a comma for a period, I may assemble the structure improperly. But this is only one kind of reading in the vast arena of what it means to respond to a text and act on it.

Classroom instruction follows the test, and up to this point the basal reader has been the test's best friend. Because the child is prepared for the five-meter sprint, books written by the best writers of our time are successfully bypassed.

Our tests cannot find out which children can read a book through to the end or give several possible interpretations of a text. Machine testing doesn't allow it. Nor can tests identify the lifetime reader.

Basically, tests help give composite profiles of children in a class or a whole school, but rarely are they able to give information worth using for instruction. An upset over a four- to six-month gain, instead of a full year, on a test in reading comprehension isn't worth considering, yet parents and teachers have often been forced into unnecessary debate over such matters.

ACTION: HELP CHILDREN LEARN HOW TO TAKE TESTS.

How well I remember the tests I used to administer as a teacher. The poor students were treated as if they were attending their own public beheading. "All right, clear your desks," I would announce in funereal tones. "No talking allowed. Have a sharp pencil. Better have a backup just in case." I fingered a stopwatch with a long dangling cord that all might see how seriously time was to be used. Most devastating to the students, I think, was my deliberate attempt to create a sense of mystery and terror, but, above all, mystery. I wanted them to think that tests were unpredictable and could aim at areas of knowledge and ability where they were least expecting it.

Today I strongly advocate preparing children to understand tests and testing through extensive class discussion about the makeup of the test and how to take it, and then adequate practice to find out their own particular weaknesses in approaching tests. Whether I agree with tests or not is immaterial. Children will take them throughout their lives, from first-grade readiness tests through the Graduate Record Examination. They are a fact of school life, and children ought to know everything they can about them.

Try some of these approaches with your children:

- Tell several stories about taking tests in your own career as a student, both positive and negative.
- Encourage children to tell their own stories about taking tests, again stressing both positive and negative.
- Ask, "What do you wonder about tests? I'll answer your questions the best I can, but I may have to go to others for help." (If you can, bring in someone who can explain tests and why they are administered.) Show children how they are put together.
- Take a sample paragraph selection and read it together; have the children answer the questions. Then have the children share their strategies for approaching the task. Show how you approached the same task.
- When the children are old enough to understand, show

them how you use time during a test—perhaps skipping over questions and materials that are difficult and returning to answer those questions later.

- Children from other cultures may react differently to the institution of testing than those raised in the Western tradition of testing. Above all, try to uncover the understanding of testing within their culture (in some cultures testing is considered a competitive act, and it is therefore poor etiquette to do well).

This is a short list. You will think of many other ways to help children understand the institution of testing, how it relates to them personally, and how they can function more effectively in taking the tests themselves.

ACTION: TAKE THE INITIATIVE; SHARE YOUR DATA WITH ADMINISTRATORS.

Administrators are forced to live complex lives, caught between parents, teachers, other administrators, school board members, and the public. They need to document the progress of the students in their schools. They need information. It is up to you to take the initiative and provide it.

During the first week of school, write up a short memo asking for an evaluation conference in October. Evaluation conferences prior to that time are usually premature. The subject of the conference is to discuss the progress of your students, your approach to evaluation in light of your understanding of what it means to be literate, and your concerns about the children's learning. By scheduling the conference in this way, you serve notice to the administrator that you are serious about evaluation and that you think six weeks into the school year is an appropriate time to discuss the children. If you can, try to arrange to have at least forty-five minutes for the session.

Include the following data in your session with the administrator:

- Your evaluation design (include the pyramid of large and small group data).
- Your evaluation process for the students who concern you most. (If possible, arrange to have the teacher with whom you reviewed your toughest cases present at the conference.)
- Children's record keeping, which shows how they actively participate in assessing their own progress, and your explanation of why this philosophy is important.
- Children's progress with conventions.
- Five or six major victories the children have experienced. (Depending on the administrator, it is often appropriate for children to talk about their breakthroughs directly.)
- The details of progress in two cases. Including these cases is as instructional to you as to the administrator. Few administrators are prepared to assess the collected work of children.
- Children's potential.

As part of any conference with a colleague, administrator, or parent be prepared to ask questions of your own with an open, inquiring tone. Some of the following questions help clarify the philosophy of the other person:

- Would you please describe the good reader/writer?
- What kind of learner do we hope to develop in this school?
- What kinds of responsibilities should the children be able to take?
- Describe what the good learner is going to need to be effective in the twenty-first century.

I often find it difficult to discuss matters of evaluation unless the other person has done some previous thinking about the function of reading and writing.

ACTION: MAKE EVALUATION A CELEBRATION OF LEARNING
WITH CHILDREN.

The entire process of evaluation ought to be a celebration of what you and the children have learned together: "I found this out." "I now know this." "Listen to this story." Indeed, the classroom ought to be filled with learning stories that contain the details of how children tried new things. Perhaps the experiments didn't work. No matter. If we examine them carefully we see the learning.

Most of the time we fall short of our plans. This is the time for reformulating how we can more effectively acquire the skill, process, or knowledge. "What do you plan to learn next? What do you think you need to learn in order to be a better reader/writer?" should be questions that signal a quest, a new journey, not a sad statement of deficit. "This is what I learned" ought to be common parlance in your classroom and mine.

Sometimes you will want to highlight celebrations. You might provide a bulletin board that calls attention each week to a major experiment or risk taken by a child in your classroom. Have children list their plans for new learning in their reading/writing folders.

FINAL REFLECTION   Most standardized assessments do not take into account new definitions of literacy, particularly the ones I have described here. It is all the more important for us to have our own data to show how children are progressing.

As much as *we* need the data to understand children's growth in reading and writing, our children need the information even more. Children spend 99 percent of their time with the book they read or the piece they write. If they do not understand their own evaluation role, they lose many opportunities for learning. Children are valuable participants in the evaluation process.

We use time differently when we delegate more evaluative responsibilities to the children. Rather than carry home piles of papers to correct, I can keep tabs on the child's effective use of folders and portfolios, and the fulfillment of personal objectives.

Evaluation in my classroom, however, must begin with a careful assessment of my own literate engagement. I cannot expect of children what I do not practice myself. I simply won't see the opportunities for children to exercise responsibility if I am not aware from my own practice what is involved in the process.

Ultimately, evaluation should be a celebration. Joint evaluation with the children more clearly gives us cause to celebrate. We take risks. We achieve objectives. We rejoice together.

references

Atwell, Nancie, 1987. *In the Middle: Writing, Reading, and Learning with Adolescents.* Portsmouth, N.H.: Boynton/Cook.

Bridwell, Norman. 1972. *Clifford Gets a Job.* New York: Scholastic.

———. 1985. *Clifford at the Circus.* New York: Scholastic.

Cleary, Beverly. 1950. *Henry Huggins.* New York: Morrow Junior Books.

Comstock, Mary, and Mary Ann Wessells. 1989. "Reading and Writing Outside the Schoolhouse: Children Explore Adult Literacy." Unpublished manuscript.

Dahl, Roald. 1986. *Matilda.* New York: Penguin.

First, Joan M. 1988. "Immigrant Students in U.S. Public Schools: Challenges with Solutions." *Phi Delta Kappan* 70 (November): 205–10.

Fox, Paula. 1985. *One-Eyed Cat.* New York: Dell.

Giacobbe, Mary Ellen. 1981. "Kids Can Write the First Week of School." *Learning* 10 (2):130–32.

Graves, Donald H. 1983. *Writing: Teachers and Children at Work.* Portsmouth, N.H.: Heinemann.

———. 1989a. *Experiment with Fiction.* The Reading/Writing Teacher's Companion Series. Portsmouth, N.H.: Heinemann.

———. 1989b. *Investigate Nonfiction.* The Reading/Writing Teacher's Companion Series. Portsmouth, N.H.: Heinemann.

———. 1989c. "When Children Respond to Fiction." *Language Arts* 66 (7) (November): 776–83.

———. 1990. *Discover Your Own Literacy.* The Reading/Writing Teacher's Companion Series. Portsmouth, N.H.: Heinemann.

Hinton, S. E. 1967. *The Outsiders.* New York: Penguin.

Hubbard, Ruth. 1985. "A Day in the Life of . . ." In *Teachers and Learners, Vol. II*, pp. 155–56. Durham, N.H.: Writing Lab, University of New Hampshire.

Li, Xiao Ming. 1989. *The Mending of the Sky and Other Chinese Myths.* Durham, N.H.: Oyster River Press.

McCord, Jean. 1968. "My Teacher the Hawk." In *Deep Where the Octopi Lie.* New York: Holt, Rinehart & Winston.

McCullagh, James C. 1984. *The Complete Book of Bicycle Fitness.* New York: Warner Books.

Naisbitt, John, and Patricia Aburdene. 1985. *Reinventing the Corporation.* New York: Warner Books.

Parsons, Frances Theodora. 1961. *How to Know the Ferns.* New York: Dover.

Peters, Thomas J., and Robert H. Waterman, Jr. 1982. *In Search of Excellence.* New York: Harper & Row.

Rief, Linda. 1984. "Writing and Rappelling: A Matter of Fear and Trust." *Learning* 13(2)(September): 72–76.

Sacks, Oliver. 1985. *The Man Who Mistook His Wife for a Hat.* New York: Summit Books.

Schnitzler, Arthur. 1982. *Anatol.* Portsmouth, N.H.: Heinemann.

Selzer, Richard. 1979. *Confessions of a Knife.* New York: Simon and Schuster.

Smith, Frank. 1982. *Writing and the Writer.* New York: Holt, Rinehart & Winston.

Thomas, Lewis. 1984. *Late-Night Thoughts on Listening to Mahler's Ninth Symphony.* New York: Bantam.

Tolstoy, Leo. 1980. *Anna Karenina.* New York: Oxford University Press.

———. 1982. *War and Peace.* New York: Penguin.

Vygotsky, Lev. 1962. *Thought and Language.* Cambridge, Mass.: The M.I.T. Press.

Vygotsky, L. S. 1978. *Mind in Society.* Cambridge, Mass.: Harvard University Press.

Wallace, Robert. 1982. *Writing Poems.* Boston: Little, Brown.

White, E. B. 1945. *Stuart Little.* New York: Harper & Row.

———. 1952. *Charlotte's Web.* New York: Harper & Row.

Wiener, Norman. 1967. *Leo Tolstoy—On Education*. Chicago: University of Chicago Press.

Williams, William Carlos. 1961. *The Farmer's Daughter*. New York: New Directions.

Wright, Carol von Pressentin. 1983. *Blue Guide of New York*. London: Ernest Benn.

Yekimov, Boris. 1989. "A Greeting from Afar." In *The Human Experience: Contemporary American and Soviet Fiction and Poetry*, ed. by the Soviet/American Joint Editorial Board of the Quaker US/USSR Committee. New York: Alfred A. Knopf; Moscow: Khudozhestvennaya Literatura.

index